ESSENTIALS

of Corporate Performance Measurement

Essentials Series

The Essential Series was created for busy business advisory and corporate professionals. The books in this series were designed so that these busy professionals can quickly acquire knowledge and skills in core business areas.

Each book provides need-to-have fundamentals for those professionals who must:

- Get up to speed quickly, because they have been promoted to a new position or have broadened their responsibility scope

- Manage a new functional area

- Brush up on new developments in their area of responsibility

- Add more value to their company or clients

Other books in this series include:

For more information on any of the above titles, please visit www.wiley.com.

ESSENTIALS

of Corporate Performance Measurement

George T. Friedlob
Lydia L. F. Schleifer
Franklin J. Plewa Jr.

John Wiley & Sons, Inc.

ISBN 0-471-20375-0

Printed in the United States of America.

10 9 8 7 6 5 4 3 2 1

Contents

Preface

The usual purpose of investing is to earn a return on that investment. The most common way to evaluate the success of investments is by measuring the return on investment (ROI). ROI is a better measure of profitability and management performance than profit itself because ROI considers the investment base required to generate profit.

The primary objectives in this book are to

1. Explain the meaning of ROI and its components

2. Describe the use of ROI to analyze performance and contribute to decision making

3. Describe various forms of ROI and how they are used to evaluate investment activities

4. Describe ways to analyze sales revenues, costs, profits, and investment centers

5. Describe recent developments in ROI: return on information technology (ROIT) and return on technology investment (ROTI);

6. Describe residual performance measures such as residual income return on investment and economic value added (EVA).

Chapter 1 introduces the concept of ROI. Chapter 2 discusses the use of ROI to analyze performance through the examination of components of ROI such as profit margin and asset turnover. The chapter also discusses the relationship of return on equity and return on investment. Chapter 3 expands on the use of ROI in decision making.

Variations of ROI can be used to improve decision making and to evaluate segments and managers.

Chapter 4 examines the gross margin return on investment (GMROI), the contribution margin return on investment (CMROI), and the cash return on investment. It also introduces the idea of quality of earnings. Chapter 5 goes into the analysis of sales revenues, costs, and profits, including an extensive discussion of several types of variances.

Chapter 6 discusses the use of ROI in evaluating investment centers, including the impact of transfer pricing. Chapter 7 discusses recent developments in ROI analysis: return on technology investments (ROTI) and return on information technology (ROIT). The chapter examines the relationship between technology and business processes and value chains.

Finally, Chapter 8 discusses an alternative approach to ROI: the use of residual income return on investment. The chapter also includes concepts related to economic value added (EVA).

Our intention is to provide a convenient and useful reference that helps you to understand how ROI can help you measure performance of companies, managers, and segments, so that you can make better decisions. We wish you success in your business ventures.

George T. Friedlob
Lydia L. F. Schleifer
Franklin J. Plewa Jr.

Acknowledgments

We wish to thank the editors at John Wiley and Sons: John De Remigis, Judy Howarth, and Alexia Meyers. We'd also like to thank one of the world's most supportive spouses, Paul Schleifer, who put in many hours of computer work on this project.

ESSENTIALS

of Corporate Performance Measurement

CHAPTER 1

The Importance of Return on Investment: ROI

After reading this chapter, you will be able to

- Understand how owners view profitability
- Compare the profitability of two companies
- Calculate a return on investment using information about profit and investment

The owners of a company and the company's creditors share a similar goal: to increase wealth. They are thus very concerned about profitability in all phases of operations. Creditors are specifically concerned that the company use its resources profitably so that it can pay interest and principal on its debt. Owners are concerned that the company be profitable so that stock values will increase. Company managers must show they can manage the owners' investment and produce the profits that owners and creditors demand. Because top management must meet the profit expectations of company owners, it passes down to the lower levels of management those profitability goals, which are then spread throughout the company. All managers, therefore, are expected to meet profitability goals, which are often increased and tightened as each level of management seeks a margin of safety.

1

The Accounting Equation

Here are two ways to view what accountants refer to as the accounting equation that relates assets and claims to assets by creditors and owners:

$$\frac{\text{Investment}}{\text{in assets}} = \frac{\text{Investment}}{\text{by creditors}} + \frac{\text{Investment}}{\text{by owners}}$$

$$\text{Assets} = \text{Debt} + \text{Owners' equity}$$

It illustrates the stake that creditors and owners have in a company's investments and explains their interest in the company's success.

What Is Profitability?

If managers are going to be held to profitability goals, someone has to figure out a way to measure *profitability*. Fortunately, accounting has. How do we measure profitability, and how do we determine standards? Is it enough for managers to report that earnings for the year are some amount such as $500,000? Earnings are determined by subtracting a company's business expenses—salaries, interest, the cost of goods sold, for example—from its revenues from sales, investments, and other sources.

Suppose that a company income statement is composed of the following:

Imaginary Company Income Statement
for the Year Ended December 31, 2002

Sales	$25,000,000
Expenses	(24,500,000)
Profit	$500,000

Our company has made half a million dollars! Does this mean that company managers have performed well? Probably not, because for sales activity of $25,000,000, owners, creditors, and top management would expect a higher profit: $500,000 is only 2 percent of $25,000,000. Business people expect that profit must be linked to activity if we are going to properly measure the adequacy of a company's profit or judge the efforts of a company's management.

Suppose Imaginary Company instead had the following income statement:

Imaginary Company Income Statement
for the Year Ended December 31, 2002

Sales	$3,125,000
Expenses	(2,625,000)
Profit	$500,000

It looks like the same half a million, but as we look at the relationship between profit and activity, where $500,000 in profits is generated by sales of $3,125,00, we can see that in this scenario the profits are 16 percent of sales.

Still, if we are going to draw conclusions about the profitability, we need to know more than the absolute dollar amount of profit ($500,000) and the relationship between profit and activity (16 percent in our example). We need to know something about how much money we are earning relative to our investment.

What Is Return on Investment?

Let's suppose that the management team for the company represented by our second income statement, with sales of $3,125,000 and profits of $500,000, runs a company with assets—plant, equipment, inventories,

3

and other items—worth $20,000,000. Does this new information change our opinion of the performance of the management team? Of course it does: $500,000 is only 2.5 percent of $20,000,000. A 2.5 percent return on an investment of $20,000,000 is not acceptable! Owners would be better off with their funds invested in treasury bills (T-bills) or even in a savings account—the return would be better, and there would be no risk. A company must generate a much higher return than T-bills or savings accounts to justify the risk involved in doing business. As our example shows, *return on investment*, or *ROI*, is calculated as follows:

$$\text{ROI} = \frac{\text{profit}}{\text{investment}}$$

$$\text{ROI} = \frac{\$500,000}{\$20,000,000} = 0.025, \text{ or 2.5 percent}$$

Let's suppose, instead, that the $500,000 profit was earned using only $2,000,000 in assets, rather than $20,000,000. ROI is now 25 percent. This return is much higher than the ROI one expects from T-bills, government bonds, or a bank savings account, and is thus much more acceptable to owners and creditors.

$$\text{ROI} = \frac{\text{profit}}{\text{investment}}$$

$$\text{ROI} = \frac{\$500,000}{\$2,000,000} = 0.25, \text{ or 25.0 percent}$$

The relationship between profit and the investment that generates the profit is one of the most widely used measures of company performance. As a quantitative measure of investment and results, ROI provides a company's management (as well as the owners and creditors) with a simple tool for examining performance. ROI allows management to cut out the guesswork and replace it with mathematical calculation, which can then be used to compare alternative uses of invested capital. (Should we increase inventory? Or pay off debt?)

Creditors and owners can always invest in government securities that yield a low rate of return but are essentially risk-free. Riskier investments require higher rates of return (reward) to attract potential investors. ROI relates profits (the rewards) to the size of the investment used to generate it.

How Can ROI Be Useful?

Profits happen when a company operates effectively. We can tell that the management team is doing its job well if the company prospers, obtains funding, and rewards the suppliers of its funds. ROI is the principal tool used to evaluate how well (or poorly) management performs.

Creditors and Owners

ROI is used by creditors and owners to do the following:

1. *Assess the company's ability to earn an adequate rate of return.* Creditors and owners can compare the ROI of a company to other companies and to industry benchmarks or norms. ROI provides information about a company's financial health.

2. *Provide information about the effectiveness of management.* Tracking ROI over a period of time assists in determining whether a company has capable management.

3. *Project future earnings.* Potential suppliers of capital assess present and future investment and the return expected from that investment.

Managers

But ROI can do more than measure a company's performance. Managers can use ROI at different levels to help them make decisions regarding how best to maximize profits and add value to the company.

Managers use ROI to do the following:

1. *Measure the performance of individual company segments when each segment is treated as an investment center.* In an investment center, each segment manager controls both profit and an investment base. ROI is the basic tool used to assess both profitability and performance.

2. *Evaluate capital expenditure proposals.* Capital budgeting is long-term planning for such items as renewal, replacement, or expansion of plant facilities. Most capital budgeting decisions rely heavily on discounted cash flow techniques.

3. *Assist in setting management goals.* Budgeting quantifies a manager's plans. Most effective approaches to goal setting use a budgeting process in which each manager participates in setting goals and standards and in establishing operating budgets that meet these goals and standards. Most budgeting efforts begin or end with a target ROI.

Summary

Perhaps the biggest reason for the popularity of ROI is its simplicity. A company's ROI is directly comparable to returns on other, perhaps more familiar, investments (such as an account at the bank) and to the company's cost of capital. If we pay 10 percent interest on capital but earn only 8 percent, that's bad. If we pay 10 percent but earn 15 percent, that's good—what could be more simple?

Alone or in combination with other measures, ROI is the most commonly used management indicator of company profit performance. It is a comprehensive tool that measures activities of different sizes and

Profit Goals May Increase as They Are Delegated

All managers are expected to meet profitability goals, which are often increased and tightened as each level of management seeks a margin of safety.

Board chair	"Let's target 5 percent profit."
President	"We need 10 percent profit this year."
Vice president	"Your goal is 15 percent."
Middle manager	"We've got to turn a 20 percent profit!"
Line manager	"Earn 25 percent or else!"

natures and allows us to compare them in a standard way. In other words, through ROI we can compare apples and oranges, at least in the area of profitability. ROI has its faults and its advantages. It is sometimes tricky to use if you do not understand it completely.

That's what we are going to do in this book—learn to understand ROI.

CHAPTER 2

Using ROI to Analyze Performance

After reading this chapter, you will be able to

- Understand the relationship between profit margin and asset turnover

- Understand the role of profit margin and asset turnover in profit planning

- Understand the relationship between return on equity and return on investment

- Understand how leverage affects the return on equity

- Understand the advantages and disadvantages of ROI

- Understand the impact on segments of using target ROIs

This ROI thing sounds sort of interesting, but who uses it? Many senior managers use ROI because it is an overall measure that is affected by a manager's activity in many different areas. Let's consider, for example, two hypothetical managers of companies that have each earned a profit of $20,000 on an investment of $100,000, to produce ROIs of 20 percent.

$$\text{Smith Company: ROI} = \frac{\$20,000}{\$100,000} = 20\%$$

$$\text{Jones Company: ROI} = \frac{\$20,000}{\$100,000} = 20\%$$

Our two managers produced the same ROI, but are their business activities otherwise the same? Is it possible that they arrived at the same ROI by completely different strategies?

Relationship between Profit Margin and Asset Turnover

Let's imagine that both companies are retail jewelers. Smith Company sells inexpensive costume jewelry in malls throughout the country. Smith Company follows a high-volume, low-markup approach to marketing. Thus, the profit margin on Smith Company sales is only 4 percent, calculated as follows:

$$\textbf{Profit margin on sales} = \frac{\textbf{profit}}{\textbf{sales}} = \frac{\$20,000}{\$500,000} = .04$$

Smith Company turns its assets over rapidly. Although asset turnover is a somewhat intuitive concept, analysts calculate it by dividing an asset into the best measure of the asset's activity. Sales is the best measure of the activity of total assets. If Smith Company creates sales of $500,000 with its investment of $100,000, its asset turnover is 5 times per year, calculated as follows:

$$\textbf{Smith Company investment turnover} = \frac{\textbf{sales}}{\textbf{investment}} = \frac{\$500,000}{\$100,000} = \textbf{5 times}$$

We can see that the ROI generated by Smith Company (20 percent) is the product of Smith Company's investment turnover (5 times) and its profit margin on sales (.04). The investment turnover is a measure of how active Smith Company has been. The profit margin on sales is a measure of how profitable that activity has been. Because Smith Company is very active, the profit margin on each sale can be low.

ROI = Investment turnover × Profit margin on sales

$$\text{ROI} = \frac{\text{sales}}{\text{investment}} \times \frac{\text{profit}}{\text{sales}} = \frac{\text{profit}}{\text{investment}}$$

$$\text{ROI} = \frac{\$500,000}{\$100,000} \times \frac{\$20,000}{\$500,000} = \frac{\$20,000}{\$100,000} = 20\%$$

$$\text{ROI} = 5 \text{ times} \times .04 = 20\%$$

Jones Company does not operate the same as Smith Company. Jones Company sells expensive, one-of-a-kind jewelry containing large diamonds and other precious stones. Because each piece is unique, Jones Company has low asset activity (turnover) and sells only a small volume of jewelry, but with high profit on each sale. As a result, Jones Company turns its assets over only 1.25 times per year.

$$\frac{\text{Investment}}{\text{turnover}} = \frac{\text{sales}}{\text{investment}} = \frac{\$125,000}{\$100,000} = 1.25 \text{ times}$$

Because Jones Company turns its assets over more slowly than Smith Company, Jones Company needs a higher profit margin on sales than Smith Company if it is to generate the same ROI. The profit margin on sales for Jones Company is 16 percent. With this markup, Jones Company achieves the same ROI of 20 percent that Smith Company achieved, but by a different combination of turnover (activity) and margin (profitability).

ROI = Investment turnover × Profit margin on sales

$$\text{ROI} = 5 \text{ times} \times .04 = .20 \text{ percent}$$

$$\text{ROI} = 1.25 \text{ times} \times .16 = .20 \text{ percent}$$

A manager who wants to increase the company's ROI must look at both factors, activity and margin. Could, for instance, the manager of Smith Company increase ROI if asset turnover increased to 5.5 times per year as a result of lowering the profit margin on sales to 3.0 percent?

$$5.5 \text{ times} \times .03 = .165$$

No, that will not work. ROI would decrease to 16.5 percent. But the manager can calculate the profit margin necessary to increase ROI to a targeted 22 percent with a turnover of 5.5 times per year.

$$5.5 \text{ times} \times \text{profit} = .22 \text{ target ROI}$$

$$\text{Margin} = \frac{.22 \text{ target ROI}}{5.5 \text{ times}} = .04$$

The manager must turn assets 5.5 times with a .04 profit margin on sales in order to generate a 22 percent ROI.

Coca-Cola and Ford

Even though two companies might be in different industries, they can still demonstrate the phenomena just discussed. Coca-Cola Bottling and Ford (the automotive division) had nearly the same ROIs in 2000. The income statements and balance sheets of these two companies are in Exhibits 2.1a–b and 2.2a–b. Their ROIs are calculated using net operating income as the return. *Operating income* is a company's income from its regular business operations. Operating income is thought to be a better measure of the earnings that a company can continue year after year, than is net income, which is affected by unusual gains and losses or changes in debt and interest expense.

$$\text{Coca-Cola ROI} = \frac{\text{profit (net operating system)}}{\text{investment}} = \frac{\$62,207}{\$1,062,097} = .0586$$

$$\text{Ford Motor ROI} = \frac{\text{profit (net operating system)}}{\text{investment}} = \frac{\$5,226}{\$95,343} = .0548$$

As we have already seen, companies can generate similar ROIs in quite different ways. So how did Coca-Cola and Ford create these returns? What strategies did their managers take? Let's separate the ROIs

EXHIBIT 2.1A

Coca-Cola's Income Statement*

	Fiscal Year		
	2000	**1999**	**1998**
In Thousands (Except Per Share Data)			
Net sales (includes sales to Piedmont of $69,539, $68,046, and $69,552)	$995,134	$972,551	$928,502
Cost of sales, excluding depreciation shown below (includes $53,463, $56,439, and $55,800 related to sales to Piedmont)	530,241	543,113	534,919
Gross margin	464,893	429,438	393,583
Selling, general and administrative expenses, excluding depreciation shown below	323,223	291,907	276,245
Depreciation expense	64,751	60,567	37,076
Amortization of goodwill and intangibles	14,712	13,734	12,972
Restructuring expense		2,232	
Income from operations	62,207	60,998	67,290
Interest expense	53,346	50,581	39,947
Other income (expense), net	974	(5,431)	(4,098)
Income before income taxes	9,835	4,986	23,245
Income taxes	3,541	1,745	8,367
Net income	$6,294	$3,241	$14,878
Basic net income per share	$ .72	$ .38	$ 1.78
Diluted net income per share	$ .71	$ .37	$ 1.75
Weighted average number of common shares outstanding	8,733	8,588	8,365
Weighted average number of common shares outstanding— assuming dilution	8,822	8,708	8,495

*(amounts in millions)

13

EXHIBIT 2.1B

Coca–Cola Balance Sheet

In Thousands (Except Share Data)

ASSETS

Current assets:

Cash

Accounts receivable, trade, less allowance for doubtful accounts
of $918 and $850

Accounts receivable from The Coca-Cola Company

Accounts receivable, other

Inventories

Prepaid expenses and other current assets

    Total current assets

Property, plant and equipment, net

Leased property under capital leases, net

Investment in Piedmont Coca-Cola Bottling Partnership

Other assets

Identifiable intangible assets, net

Excess of cost over fair value of net assets of businesses
acquired, less accumulated amortization of $35,585 and $33,141

    Total

        LIABILITIES AND STOCKHOLDERS' EQUITY

        Current liabilities:

        Portion of long-term debt payable within one year

        Current portion of obligations under capital leases

        Accounts payable and accrued liabilities

        Accounts payable to The Coca-Cola Company

        Due to Piedmont Coca-Cola Bottling Partnership

        Accrued interest payable

          Total current liabilities

        Deferred income taxes

        Other liabilities

        Obligations under capital leases

	Dec. 31, 2000	Jan. 2, 2000
	$8,425	$9,050
	62,661	60,367
	5,380	6,018
	8,247	13,938
	40,502	41,411
	14,026	13,275
	139,241	144,059
	429,978	468,110
	7,948	10,785
	62,730	60,216
	60,846	61,312
	284,842	305,783
	76,512	58,127
	$1,062,097	$1,108,392
	$ 9,904	$ 28,635
	3,325	4,483
	80,999	96,008
	3,802	2,346
	16,436	2,736
	10,483	16,830
	124,949	151,038
	148,655	124,171
	76,061	73,900
	1,774	4,468

continues

EXHIBIT 2.1B

COCA-COLA'S BALANCE SHEET CONTINUED

Long-term debt
    Total liabilities

Commitments and Contingencies (Note 11)

Stockholders' Equity:
Convertible Preferred Stock, $100 par value: Authorized—
    50,000 shares; Issued—None
Nonconvertible Preferred Stock, $100 par value: Authorized—
    50,000 shares; Issued—None
Preferred Stock, $.01 par value: Authorized—20,000,000
    shares; Issued—None
Common Stock, $1 par value: Authorized—30,000,000 shares;
    Issued—9,454,651 and 9,454,626 shares
Class B Common Stock, $1 par value: Authorized—
    10,000,000 shares; Issued 2,969,166
    and 2,969,191 shares
Class C Common Stock, $1 par value: Authorized—2
    0,000,000 shares; Issued—None
Capital in excess of par value
Accumulated deficit

Less—Treasury stock, at cost:
    Common—3,062,374 shares
    Class B Common—628,114 shares
    Total stockholders' equity
Total

---

into their investment turnover and profit margin components. Ford has an asset turnover of more than 1.5 times that of Coca-Cola, while Coca-Cola has a profit margin on sales 1.7 times that of Ford. Ford followed a strategy of more active asset use; Coca-Cola had more profitable sales. (The details of these calculations are in Exhibit 2.3.)

	Dec. 31, 2000	Jan. 2, 2000
	682,246	723,964
	1,033,685	1,077,541
	9,454	9,454
	2,969	2,969
	99,020	107,753
	(21,777)	(28,071)
	89,666	92,105
	60,845	60,845
	409	409
	28,412	30,851
	$1,062,097	$1,108,392

ROI	**= Investment turnover × Profit margin**			
Coca-Cola ROI =	.937 times	×	.063	= .058
Ford Motor ROI =	1.4813 times	×	.037	= .055

EXHIBIT 2.2A

Ford's Income Statement*

AUTOMOTIVE

Sales (Note 1)

Costs and expenses (Notes 1 and 19)

Costs of sales

Selling, administrative and other expenses

   Total costs and expenses

Operating income

Interest income

Interest expense

   Net interest income

Equity in net income/(loss) of affiliated companies (Note 1)

Net income/(expense) from transactions with Financial Services (Note 1)

Income before income taxes—Automotive

FINANCIAL SERVICES

Revenues (Note 1)

Costs and expenses (Note 1)

Interest expense

Depreciation

Operating and other expenses

Provision for credit and insurance losses

   Total costs and expenses

Net income/(expense) from transactions with Automotive (Note 1)

Gain on spin-off of The Associates (Note 19)

Income before income taxes—Financial Services

*For the Years Ended December 31, 2000, 1999, and 1998 (in millions, except amounts per share)

2000	1999	1998
$141,230	$135,073	$118,017
126,120	118,985	104,616
9,884	8,874	7,834
136,004	127,859	112,450
5,226	7,214	5,567
1,488	1,418	1,325
1,383	1,347	795
105	71	530
(70)	35	(64)
6	(45)	(191)
5,267	7,275	5,842
28,834	25,585	25,333
9,519	7,679	8,036
9,408	9,254	8,589
4,971	4,653	4,618
1,963	1,465	1,798
25,861	23,051	23,041
(6)	45	191
—	—	15,955
2,967	2,579	18,438

continues

19

EXHIBIT 2.2A

FORD'S INCOME STATEMENT CONTINUED

TOTAL COMPANY
Income before income taxes
Provision for income taxes (Note 10)
Income before minority interests
Minority interests in net income of subsidiaries
Income from continuing operations
Income from discontinued operation (Note 2)
Loss on spin-off of discontinued operation (Note 2)
Net income
Income attributable to Common and Class B Stock after Preferred
    Stock dividends (Note 1)
Average number of shares of Common and Class B Stock outstanding
    (Note 1)

AMOUNTS PER SHARE OF COMMON AND CLASS B STOCK (Note 1)
Basic income
    Income from continuing operations
    Net income
Diluted income
    Income from continuing operations
    Net income
Cash dividends

Ford Motor Company Segmental ROI Analysis

Even within a particular company that has different segments, there can
be a difference in the use of assets. Ford, for instance, did not follow the
same strategy in all parts of the company because different industries
demand different combinations of activity and margin. Exhibit 2.4 contains Ford's disclosure in the notes to its financial statements of the performance of its Automotive, Ford Credit, and Hertz segments. The
segmental and total ROI, turnover, and margin ratios (based on income
from continuing operations and average total assets) are as follows:

	2000	1999	1998
	8,234	9,854	24,280
	2,705	3,248	2,760
	5,529	6,606	21,520
	119	104	152
	5,410	6,502	21,368
	309	735	703
	(2,252)	—	—
	$3,467	$7,237	$22,071
	$3,452	$7,222	$21,964
	1,483	1,210	1,211
	$3.66	$5.38	$17.59
	2.34	5.99	18.17
	$3.59	$ 5.26	$17.19
	2.30	5.86	17.76
	$1.80	$1.88	$1.72

ROI = Investment turnover × Profit margin

Automotive ROI =	**1.445**	×	**.025**	**= .036**
Ford Credit ROI =	**.143**	×	**.065**	**= .009**
Hertz ROI =	**.490**	×	**.070**	**= .034**
Total ROI (from three segments) =	**.613**	×	**.032**	**= .020**

Ford's Automotive and Hertz segments have a greater ROI than the company as a whole; the Ford Credit segment's ROI is lower. The

EXHIBIT 2.2B

Ford's Balance Sheet*

ASSETS

Automotive

Cash and cash equivalents

Marketable securities (Note 4)

   Total cash and marketable securities

Receivables

Deferred income taxes

Other current assets (Note 1)

Current receivable from Financial Services (Note 1)

   Total current assets

Equity in net assets of affiliated companies (Note 1)

Net property (Note 9)

Deferred income taxes

Net assets of discontinued operation (Note 2)

Other assets (Note 1)

   Total Automotive assets

Financial Services

Cash and cash equivalents

Investments in securities (Note 4)

Finance receivables (Notes 5 and 7)

Net investment in operating leases (Notes 6 and 7)

Other assets

Receivable from Automotive (Note 1)

   Total Financial Services assets

   Total assets

*as of December 31, 2000 and 1999 (in millions)

	2000	1999
	$3,374	$2,793
	13,116	18,943
	16,490	21,736
	4,685	5,267
	2,239	3,762
	5,318	3,831
	1,587	2,304
	37,833	42,584
	2,949	2,539
	37,508	36,528
	3,342	2,454
	—	1,566
	13,711	13,530
	95,343	99,201
	1,477	1,588
	817	733
	125,164	113,298
	46,593	42,471
	12,390	11,123
	2,637	1,835
	189,078	171,048
	$284,421	$270,249

continues

EXHIBIT 2.2B

FORD'S BALANCE STATEMENT CONTINUED

LIABILITIES AND STOCKHOLDERS' EQUITY
Automotive
Trade payables
Other payables
Accrued liabilities (Note 11)
Income taxes payable
Debt payable within one year (Note 13)
  Total current liabilities

Long-term debt (Note 13)
Other liabilities (Note 11)
Deferred income taxes
Payable to Financial Services (Note 1)
  Total Automotive liabilities

Financial Services
Payables
Debt (Note 13)
Deferred income taxes
Other liabilities and deferred income
Payable to Automotive (Note 1)
  Total Financial Services liabilities

Company-obligated mandatorily redeemable preferred securities of a
  subsidiary trust holding solely junior subordinated debentures of
  the Company (Note 1)
Stockholders' equity
Capital stock (Notes 14 and 15)
  Preferred Stock, par value $1.00 per share (aggregate liquidation
  preference of $177 million)
  Common Stock (par value $0.01 and $1.00 per share as of 2000
  and 1999, respectively; 1.837 and 1.151 million shares issued
    as of 2000 and 1999, respectively) (Note 3)

	2000	1999
	$ 15,075	$ 14,292
	4,011	3,778
	23,515	18,488
	449	1,709
	277	1,338
	43,327	39,605
	11,769	10,398
	30,495	29,283
	353	1,223
	2,637	1,835
	88,581	82,344
	5,297	3,550
	153,510	139,919
	8,677	7,078
	7,486	6,775
	1,587	2,304
	176,557	159,626
	673	675
	*	*
	18	1,151

continues

EXHIBIT 2.2B

FORD'S BALANCE STATEMENT CONTINUED

Class B Stock, par value $0.01 and $1.00 per share as of 2000
and 1999, respectively (71 million shares issued) (Note 3)
Capital in excess of par value of stock
Accumulated other comprehensive loss
ESOP loan and treasury stock
Earnings retained for use in business
  Total stockholders' equity
  Total liabilities and stockholders' equity

---

automotive segment had an asset turnover 10 times as high as the credit segment. But the credit segment had a higher profit margin. What if the automotive segment could generate the same margin as credit; what would its ROI be then? The automotive segment would greatly increase its ROI if it could improve its margin to equal that of the credit segment.

$$\text{Automotive ROI} = \text{Investment turnover} \times \text{Profit margin}$$
$$\text{(with increased}$$
$$\text{margin)} = 1.445 \times .065 = .094$$

The DuPont Method

The DuPont system of financial control is an ROI-based management system that begins, as we just did, by separating ROI into its turnover and margin components. Each component is then separated into its own components, and those components into their components, and so forth. For example, margin is made up of two components, *profit* and *sales*. Sales is the product of price and quantity components, and profit the result of subtracting many kinds of expenses from revenues. The "In

	2000	1999
	1	71
	6,174	5,049
	(3,432)	(1,856)
	(2,035)	(1,417)
	17,884	24,606
	18,610	27,604
	$284,421	$270,249

EXHIBIT 2.3

Ratio Calculations
for Coca-Cola and Ford

ROI = Investment turnover × Profit margin

Coca-Cola ROI = $\dfrac{\text{sales}}{\text{investment}}$ × $\dfrac{\text{profit}}{\text{sales}}$

$\qquad = \dfrac{\$995,134}{\$1,062,097}$ × $\dfrac{\$62,207}{\$995,134}$ = .0586

$\qquad = $ .9370 times × .0625 = .0586

Ford Motor ROI = $\dfrac{\text{sales}}{\text{investment}}$ × $\dfrac{\text{profit}}{\text{sales}}$

$\qquad = \dfrac{\$141,230}{\$95,343}$ × $\dfrac{\$5,226}{\$141,230}$ = .0548

$\qquad = $ 1.4813 times × .0370 = .0548

EXHIBIT 2.4

Ford Motor Company's Note Disclosure of the Performance of Its Automotive, Ford Credit, and Hertz Segments

NOTE. Segment Information

Ford has identified three primary operating segments: Automotive, Ford Credit, and Hertz. Segment selection was based upon internal organizational structure, the way in which these operations are managed and their performance evaluated by management and Ford's Board of Directors, the availability of separate financial results, and materiality considerations. Segment detail is summarized as follows (in millions):

	Automotive
2000	
Revenues	
External customer	$141,230
Total Revenues	$145,013
Income	
Income before taxes	$5,267
Provision for income tax	1,597
Income from continuing operations	3,624
Other Disclosures	
Depreciation/amortization	$6,497
Interest income	1,649
Interest expense	1,589
Capital expenditures	7,393
Unconsolidated affiliates	
Equity in net income/(loss)	(70)
Investments in	2,949
Total assets at year-end	98,157

	Financial Services Sector			
Ford Credit	**Hertz**	**Other Fin Svcs**	**Elims/Other**	**Total**
$ 23,412	$5,057	342	23	$170,064
$ 23,606	$5,087	$496	$(4,138)	$170,064
$2,495	$581	$(109)	$—	$8,234
926	223	(41)	—	2,705
1,536	358	(35)	(73)	5,410
$7,846 a/	$ 1,504	$46	$56	$ 15,949
—	—	—	(161)	1,488
8,970	428	459	(544)	10,902
168	291	496	—	8,348
(22)	—	1	—	(91)
79	—	7	—	3,035
174,258	10,620	7,668	(6,282)	284,421

continues

EXHIBIT 2.4

FORD MOTOR COMPANY'S NOTE DISCLOSURE CONTINUED

	Automotive
1999	
Revenues	
External customer	$135,073
Intersegment	4,082
Total Revenues	$139,155
Income	
Income before taxes	$7,275
Provision for income tax	2,251
Income from continuing operations	4,986
Other Disclosures	
Depreciation/amortization	$5,244
Interest income	1,532
Capital Expenditures	1,469
Interest expense	7,069
Unconsolidated affiliates	
Equity in net income/(loss)	35
Investments in	2,539
Total assets at year-end	102,608
1998	
Revenues	
External customer	$118,017
Intersegment	3,333
Total Revenues	$121,350
Income	
Income before taxes	$5,842
Provision for income tax	1,743
Income from continuing operations	4,049
Other Disclosures	
Depreciation/amortization	$5,279
Interest income	1,340

Financial Services Sector				
Ford Credit	**Hertz**	**Other Fin Svcs**	**Elims/Other**	**Total**
$20,020	$4,695	$866	$4	$160,658
340	33	170	(4,625)	—
$20,360	$4,728	$1,036	$(4,621)	$160,658
$2,104	$560	$(85)	$ —	$9,854
791	224	(18)	—	3,248
1,261	336	(15)	(66)	6,502
$7,565 a/	$1,357	$326	$50	$14,542
—	—	—	(114)	1,418
7,193	354	633	(623)	9,026
82	351	157	—	7,659
(25)	—	—	—	10
97	—	8	—	2,644
156,631	10,137	12,427	(11,554)	270,249
$19,095	$4,241	$1,997	$ —	$143,350
208	9	272	(3,822)	—
$19,303	$4,250	$2,269	$(3,822)	$143,350
$1,812	$465	$16,161 b/	$ —	$24,280
680	188	149	—	2,760
1,084	277	16,060 b/	(102)	21,368
$7,327 a/	$ 1,212	$54	$31	$13,903
—	—	—	(15)	1,325

continues

EXHIBIT 2.4

FORD MOTOR COMPANY'S NOTE DISCLOSURE CONTINUED

	Automotive
Interest expense	999
Capital expenditures	7,252
Gain on spin-off of The Associates	—
Unconsolidated affiliates	
Equity in net income/(loss)	(64)
Investments in	2,187
Total assets at year-end	85,008

a/ Includes depreciation of operating leases only. Other types of depreciation/ amortization for Ford Credit are included in the Elims/Other column.

b/ Includes $15,955 million non-cash gain (not taxed) on spin-off of The Associates in the first quarter of 1998 (Note 19).

the Real World" section shows the best known of the formula charts used in the DuPont system to analyze or plan changes in ROI.

From this chart (or others like it), we can see that a manager's actions in many areas directly impact ROI. For example, if cash is managed poorly so that available balances are needlessly high, working capital and, hence, total investment, will also be high. As a direct result of higher investment, turnover will be lowered and ROI decreased.

The breakdown of ROI into margin and turnover has a number of advantages in profit planning. The components are shown as equally important in improving ROI. The importance of sales is explicitly recognized. When managers examine the formula charts used in the DuPont system of financial management, they see the multitude of trade-offs and choices available.

Return on Equity

Investors may be as interested in *return on equity* (ROE) as in ROI. Equity simply means *property rights* and refers to the interests of both

	Financial Services Sector				
Ford Credit	Hertz	Other Fin Svcs	Elims/Other	Total
6,910	318	1,114	(510)	8,831
67	317	120	—	7,756
—	—	15,955	—	15,955
2	—	—	—	(62)
76	—	—	—	2,263
137,248	8,873	6,181	(4,598)	232,712

owners and creditors, but the equity in ROE is defined as *shareholder equity* only. Thus, ROE measures the return on shareholders' investment in the company rather than the return on the company's investment in assets. For an investor, this is the most important return.

The Effect of Debt on the ROE

ROE differs from ROI because a company typically borrows part of its capital. Consider a company that creates a 15 percent ROI, as follows.

$$\text{ROI} = \frac{\text{profit}}{\text{investment}} = \frac{\$135,000}{\$900,000} = .15$$

If all the investment in assets ($900,000) is financed by owners, then owners' equity is also $900,000 and ROE is also 15 percent.

$$\text{ROE} = \frac{\text{profit}}{\text{equity}} = \frac{\$135,000}{\$900,000} = .15$$

But if one-third of the investment in assets is borrowed, and owners' equity is only $600,000, ROE is increased to 22.5 percent. If half

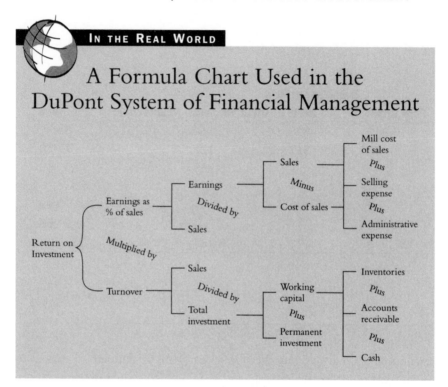

IN THE REAL WORLD

A Formula Chart Used in the DuPont System of Financial Management

the assets are from borrowed capital, ROE rises to 30 percent. At three-quarters debt, ROE is 45 percent.

The following summary calculations highlight the effect of increased debt on the ROE. As the relative amount of debt increases, the ROE also increases.

$$\text{ROE} = \frac{\text{profit}}{\text{equity}} = \frac{\$135{,}000}{\$600{,}000} = .225$$

$$\text{ROE} = \frac{\text{profit}}{\text{equity}} = \frac{\$135{,}000}{\$450{,}000} = .30$$

$$\text{ROE} = \frac{\text{profit}}{\text{equity}} = \frac{\$135{,}000}{\$400{,}000} = .45$$

The proportion of assets obtained by debt financing rather than owner investment is quite important, because debt *leverages* the owners' investment.

TIPS & TECHNIQUES

Financial Leverage as a Magnifier

Financial leverage (FL) or solvency is greater than 1.0 when a company has debt, and therefore acts like a magnifier when multiplied by the ROI to obtain the ROE.

$$ROE = ROI \times FL$$

$$= \frac{profit}{assets} \times \frac{assets}{equity}$$

$$= \frac{\$135,000}{\$900,000} \times \frac{\$900,000}{\$600,000}$$

$$= .15 \times 1.5$$

$$= .225 = 22.5\%$$

A lever placed across a fulcrum transfers pressure on the long end of the lever into a greatly magnified force on the short end, giving a powerful mechanical advantage. In the same sense, financial leverage gives a financial advantage, increasing ROE when companies borrow and then earn an ROI on the borrowed funds greater than the interest rate. Although the interest lowers earnings somewhat, the owners' investment is much smaller and the effect of earnings is magnified, increasing the return on the owners' equity (ROE). Although we omit implicit consideration of interest here, increasing debt generally increases ROE.

The Effect of Debt on Solvency

Ratios of debt and equity are called *solvency* or *leverage ratios.* Examples include debt to owners' equity, debt to total equities (debt plus owners' equity), and the inverse of these ratios. Debt and equity ratios determine the relative sizes of the property rights of creditors and owners. Too much debt restricts managers and increases the risk of owners because debt increases the fixed charges (interest expense) against income each period. Special-purpose ratios, such as the times interest earned or the fixed charge coverage ratios show the burden of fixed charges (such as interest or lease payments) and whether the company generates the earnings to pay them.

The proportion of income that interest and other fixed charges can safely consume varies from industry to industry. The ratios are used as general guidelines, similar to bank guidelines that say a consumer's house payment or car payment should be no more than a certain proportion of the consumer's income.

As the proportion of debt rises, creditors are more and more reluctant to lend. Eventually, credit will be available only at very high interest rates. Still, a certain amount of debt is good for owners because managers use debt to increase ROE, as we saw earlier.

ROI, ROE, and Solvency

We know margin times turnover equals ROI. By adding a solvency ratio, we can add information and expand these basic components to analyze ROE as well as ROI. The solvency ratio we add is total investment in assets divided by owners' equity. When we add this component to ROI, algebraically we get ROE.

$$\text{ROI} = \frac{\text{investment}}{\text{turnover}} \times \frac{\text{profit margin}}{\text{on sales}}$$

$$\text{ROE} = \frac{\text{investment}}{\text{turnover}} \times \frac{\text{profit margin}}{\text{on sales}} \times \text{solvency}$$

$$\text{ROE} = \frac{\text{sales}}{\text{investment}} \times \frac{\text{income}}{\text{sales}} \times \frac{\text{investment}}{\text{owners' equity}}$$

Returning to the examples of Coca-Cola and Ford Motor, we can determine that the ROIs, turnovers, and margins for these companies are as follows.

ROI	= investment turnover × profit margin			
Coca-Cola ROI =	.937 times	×	.063	= .059
Ford Motor ROI =	1.481 times	×	.037	= .055

Comparing Solvency Ratios

The solvency ratios for Coca-Cola and Ford Motor follow. The amounts are taken from Exhibits 2.1 and 2.2, the financial statements already shown.

$$\frac{\text{Coca-Cola}}{\text{solvency ratio}} = \frac{\text{investment}}{\text{owners' equity}} = \frac{\$1,062,097}{\$28,412} = 37.382$$

$$\frac{\text{Ford}}{\text{solvency ratio}} = \frac{\text{investment}}{\text{owners' equity}} = \frac{\$95,343}{\$6,762*} = 14.100$$

*Owner's equity = Automotive assets − Automotive liabilities

What do these ratios mean? One conclusion we draw is that Coca-Cola is much more heavily leveraged than Ford. Coca-Cola uses debt to build investment to about 37 times owners' equity, while Ford uses debt to build investment to 14 times owners' equity. The percent of investment financed by owners' equity is the inverse of the solvency ratio, 1 divided by 37.382 = 2.68 percent for Coca-Cola, and 1 divided by 14.100 = 7.09 percent for Ford. Thus, debt was used to finance 97.32 percent (1 − .0268) of the investment for Coca-Cola, 92.91 percent (1 − .0709) for Ford.

Leveraging ROE

How does this difference in leverage affect ROE? When we add leverage to our ROI components, we find Coca-Cola's 5.9 percent ROI, resulting in a 218.9 percent ROE, while Ford's only slightly lower 5.5 percent ROI is leveraged by use of debt to an ROE of only 77.3 percent.

ROE = investment turnover × profit margin × solvency						
Coca-Cola ROE =	.937 times	×	.0625	× 37.382	= 2.189
Ford Motor ROE =	1.481 times	×	.037	× 14.100	= .773

Notice how Coca-Cola and Ford Motor had similar ROIs, but their debt levels (shown by the solvency ratio) produced drastically different ROEs.

But, how typical is an ROE of 77 percent or 219 percent? When the average ROE of the Standard & Poor's 500 companies reached 20.12 percent in the first quarter of 1995—the highest level since World War II—the *Wall Street Journal* said an ROE of 20 percent was equivalent to a baseball player hitting .350.[1] But the *Wall Street Journal* was speaking of ROE calculated using *net income* after tax rather than operating earnings, as we used in our calculations. When we determine ROE using net income (the final bottom line), activities and events other than operations cause ROE for Coca-Cola to be 22.2 percent, and for Ford, 18.639 percent.

Selected financial data for Wal-Mart are included in this chapter. Using bottom-line net income, Wal-Mart's profit margin on sales is 3.3 percent, its investment turnover is 2.45, and its ratio of investment to owners' equity is 2.49. Wal-Mart's 2000 ROI is 8.06 percent and its ROE is 20.08 percent.

But some companies do even better. The 2000 balance sheet and income statement for Bristol-Myers Squibb are also included in this chapter. Again using net income rather than operating earnings, Bristol-Myers has a profit margin on sales of 25.86 percent, an investment turnover of 1.04, and a ratio of investment to owners' equity of 1.91. Bristol-Myers' ROI is 26.8 percent and its ROE is an astounding 51.4 percent.

ROE = investment turnover × profit margin × solvency

Wal-Mart ROE =	2.45	×	.033	×	2.49	=	.201
Bristol-Myers ROE =	1.04	×	.259	×	1.91	=	.514

Notice the different approaches managers use to achieve profitability in these companies in two completely different business environments: the debt levels of the two companies are not that different, but

Bristol-Myers has a very high profit margin, while Wal-Mart has a very low profit margin. Wal-Mart, however, turns over total assets (investments) about 2.5 times while Bristol-Myers turns assets (investments) only one time. Each company's strategy is appropriate to its business environment and successful in its own way.

Advantages of ROI

Managers and analysts like ROI because it is a percent and thus easy to understand and consistent with how a company measures its cost of capital. Because it is a ratio, ROI normalizes activities and makes dissimilar activities comparable. Big departments can be compared to small departments. Managers of different functions can be compared in a meaningful way. Top management uses ROI to compare segments of the company to each other, to outside companies, or to other investment opportunities. If the manager of the vacuum cleaner division creates a profit of $60,000,000 on an investment of $400,000,000, top management can compare that to the performance of the manager of the $750,000 broom division with a profit of $150,000, or to the treasurer's investment of $200,000 in a certificate of deposit at the bank.

Activity	Investment	Profit
Vacuum cleaner division	$400,000,000	$60,000,000
Broom division	750,000	150,000
Temporary investment of excess cash	200,000	14,000

These three activities, of different size and type, are difficult to compare without calculating a return on investment. Because of its flexibility, top management, financial analysts, and potential investors frequently use ROI to evaluate and compare the economic performance of companies and their segments. With the ROI of each of the activities, it is easy to rank managers' performance, as follows:

Wal–Mart Stores

The following table presents selected financial data of Wal-Mart and its subsidiaries for the periods specified.

	Fiscal Years	
	1997	**1998**
Income Statement Data		
Net sales	$104,859	$117,958
Noninterest expense	100,456	112,796
Interest expense	845	784
Total expense	101,301	113,580
Income before income taxes, minority interest, equity in unconsolidated subsidiaries and cumulative effect of accounting change	4,877	5,719
Net income	3,056	3,526

	As of	
	1997	**1998**
Balance Sheet Data		
Cash and cash equivalents	$ 883	$ 1,447
Inventories	15,897	16,497
Total current assets	17,993	19,352
Net property, plant and equipment	18,333	21,469
Net property under capital leases, net goodwill and other acquired intangible assets, and other assets and deferred charges	3,278	4,5.63
Total assets	39,604	45,384
Accounts payable	7,628	9,126
Commercial paper	—	—
Long-term debt due within one year	523	1,039
Obligations under capital leases due within one year	95	102
Total current liabilities	10,957	14,460
Long-term debt	7,709	7,191
Long-term obligations under capital leases	2,307	2,483
Total liabilities	22,461	26,881
Total shareholders' equity	17,143	18,503
Total liabilities and shareholders' equity	39,604	45,384

2000 Selected Financial Data

Ended January 31,		
1999	**2000**	**2001** (in millions)
$137,634	$165,013	$191,329
131,088	156,704	181,805
797	1,022	1,374
131,885	157,726	183,179
7,323	9,083	10,116
4,430	5,377	6,295

January 31,		
1999	**2000**	**2001** (in millions)
$ 1,879	$ 1,856	$ 2,054
17,076	19,793	21,442
21,132	24,356	26,555
23,674	32,839	37,617
5,190	13,154	13,958
49,996	70,349	78,130
10,257	13,105	15,092
—	3,323	2,286
900	1,964	4,234
106	121	141
16,762	25,803	28,949
6,908	13,672	12,501
2,699	3,002	3,154
28,884	44,515	46,787
21,112	25,834	31,343
49,996	70,349	78,130

Source: www.sec.gov

41

IN THE REAL WORLD CONTINUED

Bristol-Myers Squibb Company

(in millions except per share amounts)

	Year Ended
EARNINGS	**2000**
Net sales	$18,216
Expenses:	
Cost of products sold	4,759
Marketing, selling and administrative	3,860
Advertising and product promotion	1,672
Research and development	1,939
Special charge	—
Provision for restructuring	508
Gain on sale of business	(160)
Other	160
	12,738
Earnings from continuing operations before income taxes	5,478
Provision for income taxes	1,382
Earnings from continuing operations	4,096
Discontinued operations	
Net earnings	375
Net gain on disposal	240
	615
Net earnings	$4,711
Earnings per common share	
Basic	
Earnings from continuing operations	$2.08
Discontinued operations	
Net earnings	.19
Net gain on disposal	.13
	.32
Net earnings	$2.40
Diluted	
Earnings from continuing operations	$2.05
Discontinued operations	
Net Earnings	.19
Net gain on disposal	.12
	.31

Consolidated Statement of Earnings

December 31,	
1999	**1998**
$16,878	$15,061
4,542	3,896
3,789	3,685
1,549	1,518
1,759	1,506
—	800
—	157
—	(201)
81	62
11,720	11,423
5,158	3,638
1,369	888
3,789	2,750
378	391
—	—
378	391
$4,167	$3,141
$1.91	$1.38
.19	.20
—	—
.19	20
$2.10	$1.58
$1.87	$1.36
.19	.19
—	—
.19	.19

Bristol–Myers Squibb Company

Dollars in Millions	December 31, 2000
Assets	
Current Assets:	
Cash and cash equivalents	$3,182
Time deposits and marketable securities	203
Receivables, net of allowances	3,662
Inventories	1,831
Prepaid expenses	946
Total Current Assets	9,824
Property, plant and equipment	4,548
Insurance recoverable	262
Excess of cost over net tangible assets arising from business acquisitions	1,436
Other assets	1,508
Total Assets	$17,578
Liabilites	
Current Liabilities:	
Short-term borrowings	$162
Accounts payable	1,702
Accrued expenses	2,881
Product liability	186
U.S. and foreign income taxes payable	701
Total Current Liabilities	5,632
Other liabilities	1,430
Long-term debt	1,336
Total Liabilities	8,398
Stockholders' Equity	
Preferred stock, $2 convertible series: Authorized 10 million shares; issued and outstanding 9,864 in 2000, 10,977 in 1999 and 11,684 in 1998, liquidation value of $50 per share	—

Consolidated Balance Sheet

1999	1998
$2,720	$2,244
237	285
3,272	3,190
2,126	1,873
912	1,190
9,267	8,782
4,621	4,429
468	523
1,502	1,587
1,256	951
$17,114	$16,272
$432	$482
1,657	1,380
2,367	2,302
287	877
794	750
5,537	5,791
1,590	1,541
1,342	1,364
8,469	8,696
—	—

continues

45

IN THE REAL WORLD CONTINUED

Bristol-Myers Squibb Company

Dollars in Millions	December 31, 2000
Stockholders' Equity	
Common stock, par value of $.10 per share: Authorized 4.5 billion shares; 2,197,900,835 issued in 2000, 2,192,970,504 in 1999, and 2,188,316,808 in 1998	220
Capital in excess of par value of stock	2,002
Other comprehensive income	(1,103)
Retained earnings	17,781
	18,900
Less cost of treasury stock—244,365,726 common shares in 2000, 212,164,851 in 1999, and 199,550,532 in 1998	9,720
Total Stockholders' Equity	9,180
Total Liabilities and Stockholders' Equity	$17,578

Activity	ROI
Broom division	20%
Vacuum cleaner division	15%
Temporary investment of excess cash	7%

ROI as a Comprehensive Tool

ROI is a comprehensive measure, affected by all the business activities that normally determine financial health. ROI is increased or decreased by the level of operating expenses incurred, and by changes in either sales volume or price. The investment base can include capital investment in plant, property, and equipment, or current investments such as receivables and inventories. Many managers think ROI is useful because it provides a means of monitoring the results of capital investment deci-

Consolidated Balance Sheet, continued

1999	1998	
219	219	
1,533	1,075	
(816)	(622)	
15,000	12,540	
15,936	13,212	
7,291	5,636	
8,645	7,576	
$17,114	$16, 272	

Source: Bristol-Myers Squibb Annual Report

sions: If a project does not earn its projected return, the manager's ROI goes down.

Gearing Investment and Profit

ROI is often criticized as making a complex management process appear unrealistically simple. An ROI of 20 percent, for example, appears to mean that each $1.00 in assets provides profit of $0.20. A $1.00 reduction in assets is accompanied by a $0.20 reduction in profits; a $1.00 increase in assets by a $0.20 increase in profit. The relationship described by an ROI percentage implies that an increase or decrease in investment is geared to an increase or decrease in profits by the ROI ratio.

Summary of Advantages of ROI

- ROI is easy to understand.

- ROI is directly comparable to the cost of capital.

- ROI normalizes dissimilar activities so they can be understood.

- ROI is comprehensive, reflecting all aspects of a business.

- ROI shows the results of capital investment decisions.

Although the gearing of profit and investment is to some extent true, the relationship between investment and profit is not constant over all the assets in a segment. If, for example, Division A has an ROI of 20 percent, it seems to follow that if Division A increases its investment in inventory or equipment by $100,000, the division's return will increase by $20,000 ($100,000 × 20 percent). Likewise, if Division B has an ROI of 25 percent, an additional $100,000 investment in inventory or equipment here will return $25,000. Regardless of the type of investment—inventory, equipment, or whatever—the ROI relationship appears to predict the profit that managers can expect. But this is not true.

Different types of investment have different effects on profit. Investments required by OSHA (for safety precautions) or by the EPA (for pollution control) may have no effect whatever on profits. Other investments may individually create an array of different returns, regardless of the entity's overall ROI. An investment in high-tech robotics for production may create a much higher ROI than an investment in higher inventory stocks, for example.

Gearing investment and profit seems to imply that ROI is different in different segments for investment in identical assets (equipment or inventory, for example). The ROI for the asset appears to be determined not by its nature and use but by the ROI of the segment in which the investment is made. As we have seen, if investment and profit are linked, inventory (or any other investment) is expected to return 20 percent in Division A, but 25 percent in Division B. As a result, justifying an increase in inventory to support sales requires a larger contribution to profits in one segment than in the other.

But the change in profit that actually accompanies a change in inventory investment depends on the segment's inventory level before the change, not on the ROI of the segment's existing mix of assets. For example, if insufficient inventory levels are increased, profits might increase because stockouts are prevented and customer choice is improved. But increasing an inventory that is already at an optimum level may decrease profit as a result of increased carrying charges and obsolescence.

A series of costs fluctuate as inventory levels vary from low to high. These include the cost of stockouts and poor customer selection (at low inventory levels); the cost of insurance, taxes, and other carrying costs; and ordering and receiving costs (lower inventory levels require more orders to maintain). The total of these costs is usually greater at very low and very high inventory levels than at some intermediate, optimum level that balances the cost of stockouts against excess carrying costs. A graph in Exhibit 2.5 shows how a segment's total inventory costs might vary with inventory level. The effect of a change in inventory investment depends on the segment's position on this graph when the investment is made.

Requiring identical investments to pay their way with different returns in different segments of the company distorts the way managers make decisions. In a segment with a high ROI, for instance, there is an

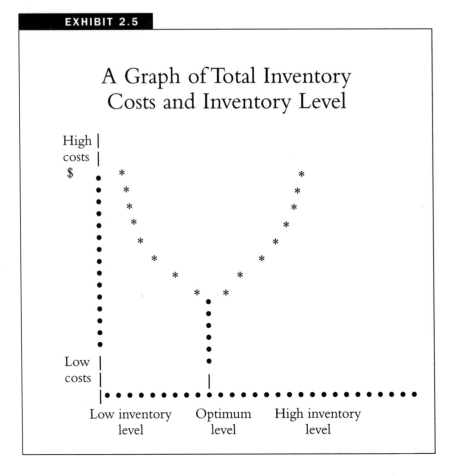

EXHIBIT 2.5

A Graph of Total Inventory
Costs and Inventory Level

incentive for managers to lease assets that create low returns, even though other segments (with lower returns) routinely purchase the same assets. Again, assume Division A has an ROI of 20 percent, and Division B an ROI of 25 percent. The cost of capital to the company is 18 percent and both divisions need new warehouses that are each expected to generate ROIs of 22 percent on the $100,000 invested. Division A will buy a warehouse because the 22 percent return will increase the segment return, but Division B will lease because the same return lowers its ROI.

	Division A	Division B
Assets	$1,000,00	$1,000,000
Profit	200,000	250,000
ROI	20%	25%
Plus new warehouse	100,000	100,000
New assets	1,100,000	1,100,000
Plus added profit	22,000	22,000
New profit	222,000	272,000
New ROI	20.18%	24.72%
Change in ROI	increased .18%	decreased .28%
Decision	buy warehouse	lease warehouse

In both cases, the return generated by the warehouse is greater than the company's cost of capital, and purchasing the warehouse would benefit the company. (From the company's perspective, a $100,000 warehouse investment yields a 22 percent return with only an 18 percent cost of capital in either case.) Division A's actions are congruent with the company's goal of increasing company profit. Division B's are not.

The Drawbacks of Targeting an ROI

In an attempt to be fair, top managers in some companies establish a single ROI target for all segment managers. But when all segments have the same target ROI, the process is unfair due to the factors just discussed. Consider, for example, a company that has four operating segments. Three of the segments are furniture stores; the fourth is the company's customer credit-granting segment.

Store A was built in 1970 with an investment of $200,000. The other two stores (B and C) were built two years ago. All three stores are identical, but due to inflation, Stores B and C each cost $600,000 to build. All the stores carry an average furniture inventory costing

$200,000. The investment in the credit-granting segment consists of $100,000 in office equipment and computers in rented offices. Each of the stores earned a profit of $80,000 for the year and the Credit Office earned $6,000.

Store	A	B	C	Credit Office
Building and equipment	$200,000	$600,000	$600,000	$100,000
Inventory	200,000	200,000	200,000	NA
Total investment	$400,000	$800,000	$800,000	$100,000
Profit	$80,000	$80,000	$80,000	$6,000
ROI	20%	10%	10%	6%

Each store has an identical building and the same amount of inventory; each generates the same profit; and still, because the assets were acquired at different times, the old and new segment ROIs are not comparable in a meaningful way. The Credit Office creates an ROI of only 6 percent, but, because of its different asset mix and the different function it serves, it cannot be compared directly to the stores. The profit of the Credit Office depends on the other three segments generating credit sales. Likewise, the profit and ROI created by the stores depend on the ability to offer credit.

Because of the different ages of the stores and because the ROIs of the furniture stores and the Credit Office are not comparable, a single ROI target for all segments is neither practical nor useful.

Accounting Methods, Timing, and Manipulation

On another level, managers might find that otherwise similar segments lack comparability because managers may use different accounting procedures, particularly for inventories and long-lived assets, that by themselves make accounting earnings different. For example, choosing last-in, first-out (LIFO) rather than first-in, first-out (FIFO) inventory accounting, or accelerated depreciation rather than straight-line, will change accounting income substantially.

Other costs are subject to manipulation. A manager might delay or eliminate some crucial but routine maintenance procedures to lower costs and improve earnings in a slow period. Likewise, discretionary costs such as advertising or research might be delayed or eliminated. Production can be increased to lower the average overhead per unit, positions that are vacated can be left unfilled, and other counterproductive measures can be taken to increase profits and ROI.

At the extreme, segment managers might falsify records, increasing inventories to reduce cost of goods sold, or recording sales in the current year even though they were made after the year-end cut-off. Accounts found to be uncollectible may be retained on the books as good receivables and spoiled or obsolete inventory included as good.

Manipulation and fraud are encouraged when top management sets unrealistic ROI targets for segment managers.

Summary

The ROI can be analyzed as the product of two components: profit margin and asset turnover. Profit margin expresses the percentage of sales a company realizes in profits. A high profit margin indicates that a company is controlling its costs relative to its sales. Asset turnover indicates how much sales the company is generating relative to its assets. A company can improve asset turnover by increasing sales or selling off nonproductive assets. Increasing the asset turnover and/or increasing the profit margin will increase the ROI.

From the stockholders' point of view, the return on equity (ROE) is a useful measure of performance. If a company increases its debt relative to its equity, the company's leverage increases. This may have the effect of increasing the company's risk, but it also will cause the company's ROE to be greater than its ROI, as long as it generates enough income to cover additional interest expense.

CHAPTER 3

ROI and Decision Making

- Understand how managers make decisions based on ROI and cost of capital

- Understand how managers might use variations of the ROI to improve decision making

- Understand the contribution of ROI in budgeting

- Understand the differences in assessing segment performance and assessing manager performance using ROI

- Understand issues regarding how to define the asset base, the relevant liabilities to deduct, and the appropriate value of assets

There are some problems with using ROI for investment decisions. A commonly cited one is the refusal of managers to pursue investments that might reduce the manager's ROI, even though they are otherwise acceptable. For example, a segment manager with a segment ROI of 25 percent might refuse to invest in a project or asset expected to return 20 percent, even if the company's cost of capital is only 15 percent, because investing in a project with a 20 percent return when the segment's ROI is 25 percent will lower segment ROI.

Before New Project		New Project	With New Project
Investment	$1,000	$250	$1,250
Profit	250	50	300
ROI	25%	20%	24%

The same type of thinking might lead a segment manager to increase ROI by disinvesting in assets that return less than the segment's ROI. Scrapping or selling otherwise profitable assets that return only 20 percent when the segment's ROI is 24 percent increases a manager's ROI.

With Low ROI Project		Project Scrapped	Without Project
Investment	$1,250	$250	$1,000
Profit	300	50	250
ROI	24%	20%	25%

In both cases, the project return is greater than the company's cost of capital and adds to the company's total dollar profit. Now, segment managers might not make the decision to scrap or sell lower-return assets because top management would probably notice the sale, but top management is less likely to notice when a segment manager passes on an investment opportunity. Top managers often learn only of opportunities disclosed to them by segment managers. If a segment manager does not present a project to the top management, they may never learn of it.

Both rejecting the 20 percent project and disinvesting in a 20 percent asset are probably not good decisions for the company viewed as a whole. But segment managers who do these things are acting rationally from their own perspective, increasing the ROI of their segments. If top management is to avoid these situations, there must be goals for segment managers other than a target or maximum ROI.

Profit-Neutral, Nondiscretionary Investments

Sometimes managers have to invest in things. These so-called nondiscretionary investments often do not create increases in profit. Examples of such profit-neutral investments include replacing or upgrading administrative or support facilities (such as buildings or parking lots) and adding equipment because of OSHA regulations or EPA requirements.

Some managers argue that because these nondiscretionary projects require capital but do not return capital, other projects must return significantly more than a company's cost of capital. Thus, pushing managers toward projects that earn substantially more than the cost of capital is beneficial because the returns of profitable operations must be sufficient to cover the cost of capital invested in nondiscretionary projects that create no returns.

If a company with a $1,000,000 investment in assets has a 15 percent cost of capital, any return above 15 percent results in profit. An ROI of 17 percent gives a profit of $170,000.

Assets	$1,000,000
Profit @ 17% ROI in assets	170,000
Cost of capital @ 15% of $1,000,000	150,000
Profit in excess of the cost of capital	20,000

But if $200,000 of the company's investment in assets is in nondiscretionary, profit-neutral projects, leaving productive assets of only $800,000, a return of 17 percent on productive assets is not enough to cover the cost of capital.

Total assets	1,000,000
Nondiscretionary profit-neutral assets	200,000
Productive assets	$800,000
Profit @ 17% ROI on productive assets	136,000
Cost of capital @ 15% of $1,000,000	(150,000)
Excess of the cost of capital over profit	14,000

If this company is to create a profit, the ROI for productive assets must be 18.75 percent or greater. A hurdle rate is the rate a project must clear to produce a positive return when all investments are considered. The hurdle rate can be equal to or greater than the cost of capital:

Productive assets	$ 800,000
Nondiscretionary profit-neutral assets	200,000
Total assets	1,000,000
Profit @ 18.75% ROI on productive assets	150,000
Cost of capital @ 15% of $1,000,000	(150,000)
Profit and the cost of capital are equal	- 0 -

Managers often make poor investment decisions using an ROI (accounting return) model rather than a discounted cash flow model. Realizing that some assets create no profit is only part of the problem.

ROI and Budgeting

Although ROI provides an incentive to managers to ignore company goals and avoid some profitable investments, the planning process can help managers resist this temptation. In their annual planning, managers first budget sales prices and quantities, then the costs of the planned sales and the other operating costs that must be incurred. Profit is determined from the budgets of sales and expenses. Next, managers determine the investment in inventory and other assets necessary to support the planned sales activity. Asset additions are usually budgeted using *net present values* (NPV) of cash flows rather than ROI targets.

When the planning process is complete, budgeted profit divided by the budgeted asset base determines the segment's target ROI. But budgeted ROI is a target only to the extent that all the budgeted items that compose it are targets. Budgeted ROI targets may be lower than the actual ROI of current and past years, thus allowing managers to accept projects with a return between the cost of capital and the segment's ROI.

When top management uses budgets to evaluate managers, they often assess the manager's ability to establish a workable budget (usually working with the manager's superior) and then accomplish the goals the budget describes. Segment managers can thus be evaluated by comparing actual ROI to budgeted ROI instead of by ranking segment ROIs. Budgeting that incorporates a target ROI allows top management to consider the profit potential of each segment and allows segment managers to invest in assets that increase residual income (RI), even if they reduce ROI.

Determining Profit and the Investment Base

With RI, ROI, and other factors involved, what should segment managers use to help them make investment decisions? If a company uses ROI to evaluate segments, the segment manager will have to decide what composition of return and investment to use. Several forms of profit and investment can be identified, depending on the goal of the evaluation. Is, for instance, top management evaluating the *economic performance of the segment* or the *managerial performance of the segment manager*? They are not the same thing. Economic performance evaluation of the segment calls for classifying certain components of profit and the asset base in a completely different manner.

If economic performance is assessed, the segment should bear all costs directly associated with its operation and all investment dedicated to its mission, regardless of who controls the costs or manages the investment base. The inclusion here of allocated costs is discretionary. If the goal is to assess the manager's performance, only the components of profit and the investment base controlled by the manager should be included.

Measuring Profit

Profit in published financial statements is determined using generally accepted accounting principles (GAAP), and the performance of segments shown in published financial statements is calculated in the same way.

Most companies provide the type of segment disclosure shown in Exhibit 3.1, which shows segment information for Ford Motor Company from its 2000 annual report. Ford Motor Company shows revenues, income from continuing operations, capital expenditures, depreciation expense, and assets for its automotive, Ford Credit, and Hertz operations. Such detail of segment disclosure allows us to calculate ROI for each of these business segments.

Ford Motor Company presents the GAAP-based information that is useful for stockholders and others in assessing the performance of the company's operating segments, but it is *not* useful in assessing the performance of segment managers. Companies that use ROI to assess the performance of managers, rather than segments, will often exclude one or more of the following in segment operating expenses: income taxes, interest on corporate debt, allocated costs (of administration or other activities), or any other costs the segment manager does not control.

Some companies argue that charging a share of interest expense to a segment makes managers aware that invested funds are not free. If there is no cost, some argue, segment managers might tend to use more funds than they otherwise would. Still, because it ignores the cost of owners' equity, an interest charge understates the true cost of capital, which includes the cost of both debt and owners' equity. (This understatement is in all income statements.) This causes others to insist that if managers realize (as they do) that invested funds must recover the unstated cost of equity capital, they also realize that the cost of creditor capital must be recovered, even in the absence of a stated interest charge.

Determining Investment Base

There are three main questions to answer in determining the investment amount to use in an ROI calculation:

- What assets should be included?
- What liabilities should be deducted?
- How should assets be valued?

The remainder of this chapter discusses these questions.

What Assets Should Be Included?

Deciding what assets to include will depend, in part, on whether top management is evaluating a segment's manager or the economic performance of the segment. The issue is much the same for investment as it is for profit. If the economic performance of the segment is assessed, segment investment should include all capital dedicated to its mission, regardless of who manages the investment. But if instead the segment manager's performance is assessed, only those components of investment controlled by the manager should be included.

But the question is broader than defining the entity to be evaluated. Another common problem is deciding on the treatment of shared assets. This is a problem analogous to allocating shared expenses in determining operating income.

EXHIBIT 3.1

Ford Motor Company Segment Disclosure from 2000 Annual Report

NOTE 21. Segment Information

Ford has identified three primary operating segments: Automotive, Ford Credit, and Hertz. Segment selection was based upon internal organizational structure, the way in which these operations are managed and their performance evaluated by management and Ford's Board of Directors, the availability of separate financial results, and materiality considerations. Segment detail is summarized as follows (in millions):

	Automotive
2000	
Revenues	
External customer	$141,230
Total Revenues	$145,013
Income	
Income before taxes	$5,267
Provision for income tax	1,597
Income from continuing operations	3,624
Other Disclosures	
Depreciation/amortization	$6,497
Interest income	1,649
Interest expense	1,589
Capital expenditures	7,393
Unconsolidated affiliates	
Equity in net income/(loss)	(70)
Investments in	2,949
Total assets at year-end	98,157

	Financial Services Sector			
Ford Credit	**Hertz**	**Other Fin Svcs**	**Elims/Other**	**Total**
$23,412	$5,057	342	23	$170,064
$23,606	$5,087	$496	$(4,138)	$170,064
$2,495	$581	$(109)	$—	$8,234
926	223	(41)	—	2,705
1,536	358	(35)	(73)	5,410
$7,846 a/	$1,504	$46	$56	$ 15,949
—	—	—	(161)	1,488
8,970	428	459	(544)	10,902
168	291	496	—	8,348
(22)	—	1	—	(91)
79	—	7	—	3,035
174,258	10,620	7,668	(6,282)	284,421

continues

EXHIBIT 3.1				

FORD MOTOR COMPANY SEGMENT DISCLOSURE CONTINUED

	Automotive
1999	
Revenues	
External customer	$135,073
Intersegment	4,082
Total Revenues	$139,155
Income	
Income before taxes	$ 7,275
Provision for income tax	2,251
Income from continuing operations	4,986
Other Disclosures	
Depreciation/amortization	$ 5,244
Interest income	1,532
Interest expense	1,469
Capital expenditures	7,069
Unconsolidated affiliates	
Equity in net income/(loss)	35
Investments in	2,539
Total assets at year-end	102,608
1998	
Revenues	
External customer	$118,017
Intersegment	3,333
Total Revenues	$121,350
Income	
Income before taxes	$ 5,842
Provision for income tax	1,743
Income from continuing operations	4,049

| | Financial Services Sector | | | |
Ford Credit	Hertz	Other Fin Svcs	Elims/Other	Total
$20,020	$4,695	$ 866	$ 4	$160,658
340	33	170	(4,625)	—
$20,360	$4,728	$ 1,036	$(4,621)	$160,658
$ 2,104	$ 560	$ (85)	$ —	$ 9,854
791	224	(18)	—	3,248
1,261	336	(15)	(66)	6,502
$ 7,565 a/	$1,357	$ 326	$ 50	$ 14,542
—	—	—	(114)	1,418
7,193	.354	.633	(623)	9,026
82	351	157	—	7,659
(25)	—	—	—	10
97	—	8	—	2,644
156,631	10,137	12,427	(11,554)	270,249
$19,095	$4,241	$ 1,997	$ —	$143,350
208	9	272	(3,822)	—
$19,303	$4,250	$ 2,269	$(3,822)	$143,350
$ 1,812	$ 465	$16,161 b/	$ —	$ 24,280
680	188	149	—	2,760
1,084	277	16,060 b/	(102)	21,368

continues

EXHIBIT 3.1

FORD MOTOR COMPANY SEGMENT DISCLOSURE CONTINUED

	Automotive
Other Disclosures	
Depreciation/amortization	$5,279
Interest income	1,340
Interest expense	999
Capital expenditures	7,252
Gain on spin-off of The Associates	—
Unconsolidated affiliates	
Equity in net income/(loss)	(64)
Investments in	2,187
Total assets at year-end	85,008

a/ Includes depreciation of operating leases only. Other types of depreciation/ amortization for Ford Credit are included in the Elims/Other column.
b/ Includes $15,955 million non-cash gain (not taxed) on spin-off of The Associates in the first quarter of 1998 (Note 19).

Shared assets can include a common pool of cash and receivables. Most companies do not include shared facilities in the investment base, but many include cash and receivables. For example, if headquarters sets company credit policy and is responsible for collecting accounts receivable, and if company cash is centrally controlled, should cash and receivables be in a segment's assets base? Because it is difficult to determine appropriate amounts of cash or receivables for each segment, some companies include cash and receivables at arbitrary amounts, such as cash equal to two week's payables, or receivables equal to two month's sales.

What Liabilities Should Be Deducted?

Regardless of the assets included, there are at least three variations of investment created by subtracting different liabilities. Each variation stems from a different conception of investment and results in a differ-

| | Financial Services Sector | | | |
Ford Credit	Hertz	Other Fin Svcs	Elims/Other	Total
$7,327 a/	$1,212	$54	$31	$13,903
—	—	—	(15)	1,325
6,910	318	1,114	(510)	8,831
67	317	120	—	7,756
—	—	15,955	—	15,955
2	—	—	—	(62)
76	—	—	—	2,263
137,248	8,873	6,181	(4,598)	232,712

ent ROI. All can be used for either the company as a whole or for segments within the company. Exhibits 3.2a and 3.2b contain the 2000 income statement and balance sheet of Abbott Laboratories. The amounts in the exhibits are used to calculate the three returns described next. In each case, we use net income as the numerator.

1. *Total assets.* This measure deducts no liabilities and gives an ROI sometimes called *return on assets*, or ROA.

Net Income	$2,785,977
Divided by total assets	$15,283,254
Equals an ROI (ROA) of	18.23%

2. *Total assets minus current liabilities.* Subtracting current liabilities from total assets gives a return on all funds committed for the

EXHIBIT 3.2A

Abbott Laboratories 2000
Income Statement
(in thousands)

Consolidated Statement of Earnings and Comprehensive Income
(dollars and shares in thousands except per share data)

Year Ended December 31

Net Sales

Cost of products sold

Research and development

Selling, general and administrative

Gain on sale of business

Total Operating Cost and Expenses

Operating Earnings

Net interest expense

Income from TAP Pharmaceutical Products Inc. joint venture

Net foreign exchange (gain) loss

Other (income) expense, net

Earnings Before Taxes

Taxes on earnings

Net Earnings

Basic Earnings Per Common Share

Diluted Earnings Per Common Share

Average Number of Common Shares Outstanding Used for Basic
    Earnings Per Common Share

Dilutive Common Stock Options

Average Number of Common Shares Outstanding Plus Dilutive
    Common Stock Options

Outstanding Common Stock Options Having No Dilutive Effect

2000	1999	1996
$13,745,916	$13,177,625	$12,512,734
6,238,646	5,977,183	5,406,635
1,351,024	1,193,963	1,228,777
2,894,176	2,657,104	2,759,757
(138,507)	—	—
10,345,341	10,028,250	9,395,169
3,400,575	3,149,375	3,117,565
23,221	81,765	102,540
(481,340)	(390,152)	(266,347)
7,287	26,238	31,158
35,000	34,636	8,349
3,816,407	3,396,888	3,241,865
1,030,430	951,129	907,512
$2,785,977	$2,445,759	$2,334,353
$1.80	$1.59	$1.52
$1.78	$1.57	$1.50
1,548,015	1,536,762	1,537,242
17,564	20,893	23,716
1,565,579	1,557,655	1,560,958
1,038	1,807	657

EXHIBIT 3.2

ABBOTT LABORATORIES 2000 INCOME STATEMENT CONTINUED

Year Ended December 31

Comprehensive Income:

Foreign currency translation adjustments

Tax benefit (expense) related to foreign currency translation adjustments

Unrealized gains (loss) on marketable equity securities

Tax benefit (expense) related to unrealized gains (loss) on marketable equity securities

Reclassification adjustment for realized gains

Tax expense related to reclassification adjustment for realized gains

Other comprehensive income (loss), net of tax

Net Earnings

Comprehensive Income

Supplemental Comprehensive Income Information:

Cumulative foreign currency translation loss adjustments, net of tax

Cumulative unrealized (gains) on marketable equity securities, net of tax

The accompanying notes to consolidated financial statements are an integral part of this statement.

2000	1999	1996
$(198,475)	$(172,517)	$1,504
(476)	1,286	441
31,252	(10,548)	1,000
(12,500)	4,171	(396)
(29,520)	—	=
11,808	—	—
(197,911)	(177,608)	2,549
2,785,977	2,445,759	2,334,353
$2,588,066	$2,268,151	$2,336,902
$630,893	$431,942	$260,711
(27,681)	(26,641)	(33,018)

EXHIBIT 3.2B

Abbott Laboratories Consolidated Balance Sheet (dollars in thousands)

December 31

Assets

Current Assets:

Cash and cash equivalents

Investment securities

Trade receivables, less allowances of—2000: $190,167;
  1999: $238,956; 1998: $191,352

Inventories—

Finished products

Work in process

Materials

Total inventories

Prepaid income taxes

Other prepaid expenses and receivables

Total Current Assets

Investment Securities

Property and Equipment, at Cost:

Land

Buildings

Equipment

Construction in progress

Less: accumulated depreciation and amortization

Net Property and Equipment

Net Intangible Assets

Deferred Charges, Investments in Joint Ventures and Other Assets

Liabilities and Shareholders' Investment

2000	1999	1996
$914,218	$608,097	$315,238
242,500	115,199	95,827
2,179,451	2,055,839	1,955,866
903,973	772,478	697,974
370,407	338,818	347,150
466,951	384,148	367,616
1,741,331	1,495,444	1,412,740
896,083	918,617	847,154
1,402,858	1,226,558	962,936
7,376,241	6,419,754	5,589,761
637,979	954,778	967,819
245,850	202,858	165,474
1,953,665	1,882,439	1,860,265
7,597,553	7,339,578	7,104,805
330,830	372,692	272,949
10,127,898	9,797,567	9,403,493
5,310,987	5,027,508	4,660,555
4,816,911	4,770,059	4,742,938
1,555,260	1,574,851	1,349,822
896,863	751,602	609,579
$15,283,254	$14,471,044	$13,259,919

EXHIBIT 3.2B

ABBOTT LABORATORIES CONSOLIDATED BALANCE SHEET CONTINUED

December 31

Current Liabilities:

Short-term borrowings and current portion of long-term debt

Trade accounts payable

Salaries, wages and commissions

Other accrued liabilities

Dividends payable

Income taxes payable

Total Current Liabilities

Long-Term Debt

Deferred Income Taxes

Other Liabilities and Deferrals

Shareholders' Investment:

Preferred shares, one dollar par value
    Authorized—1,000,000 shares, none issued

Common shares, without par value
    Authorized—2,400,000,000 shares, issued at stated capital
    amount—Shares: 2000: 1,563,436,372; 1999: 1,564,670,440;
    1998: 1,548,382,682

Common shares held in treasury, at cost—
    Shares: 2000: 17,502,239; 1999: 17,650,834; 1998:
    17,710,838

Unearned compensation—restricted stock awards

Earnings employed in the business

Accumulated other comprehensive loss

Total Shareholders' Investment

The accompanying notes to consolidated financial statements are an
integral part of this statement.

2000	1999	1996
$479,454	$896,271	$1,759,145
1,355,985	1,226,854	1,057,417
401,366	383,552	375,804
1,549,245	1,433,424	1,379,953
293,800	263,000	227,400
217,690	313,610	166,183
4,297,540	4,516,711	4,965,902
1,076,368	1,336,789	1,339,694
—	23,779	108,964
1,338,440	1,166,170	1,091,720
—	—	—
2,218,234	1,939,673	1,310,500
(255,586)	(257,756)	(46,735)
(18,116)	(23,028)	(25,796)
7,229,586	6,174,007	4,743,315
(603,212)	(405,301)	(227,693)
8,570,906	7,427,595	5,753,591
$15,283,254	$14,471,044	$13,259,919

long term. This measure of ROI is important to top management, and many (but not most) companies deduct current liabilities from a segment's asset base.

Net income		$2,785,977
Divided by:		
Total assets	$15,283,254	
Minus current liabilities	4,297,540	
		10,985,714
Equals an ROI of		25.36%

3. *Total assets minus all liabilities.* This measure gives a return on net assets or on owners' equity, sometimes called return on equity, or ROE. ROE is often used by shareholders or their analysts, and is discussed further in Chapter 2.

Net income		$ 2,785,977
Divided by:		
Total assets	$15,283,254	
Minus total liabilities	6,712,348	
		$8,570,906
Equals an ROI (ROE) of		32.51%

Some managers of large segments might be able to borrow long-term directly or manage their own short-term payables. Or a segment might even be a subsidiary with full range of long- and short-term debt. In these cases, it makes good sense to subtract from assets any debt a segment management controls. This allows the company to measure the return on its capital invested long-term in the segment. (This is done by a parent company that calculates its ROE in its subsidiary company.)

Usually, however, ROA is the ROI measure best suited to investment centers because managers most often do not know or care about the source of their funds.

How Should Assets Be Valued?

There are at least four approaches to valuing the assets included in the investment base.

1. *Gross book value.* This approach uses the historical or acquisition cost of assets, without deducting accumulated depreciation, amortization, or depletion.

2. *Net book value.* Net book value of assets is gross book value minus accumulated depreciation, amortization, and depletion. This is the most used valuation approach.

3. *Replacement cost.* Replacement cost is the estimated cost of replacing the assets. Replacement cost sounds logical but has definitional and other problems, discussed later in the chapter.

4. *Economic value.* This method uses the present value of future cash flows. Almost no one uses economic value.

Gross Book Value

Using the gross book value of the assets in the investment base gives managers an incentive to make unwise equipment disposal and replacement decisions.

Disposal Decisions.

Managers who are evaluated by an ROI using gross book values have an incentive to (1) scrap old equipment that is fully depreciated, infrequently used, but still needed, and (2) scrap any equipment that is not returning a target ROI, regardless of condition. Even if scrapping equipment is foolish from the company's viewpoint and produces a loss on disposal for the segment, the disinvestment still improves the segment's ROI because it reduces the investment base (the denominator). The disposal will improve ROI even in the year of disposal if the loss on disposal is less than the disposed asset's profit shortfall.

For example, Segment X has a piece of equipment, A, that returns less than the other assets, as follows.

SEGMENT X

	Equipment A	All Other Assets	Total for Segment
Gross BV	$100,000	$500,000	$600,000
Profit	15,000	125,000	140,000
ROI	15%	25%	23.33%

Equipment A has a profit shortfall of $10,000. (A profit of $10,000 more, or $25,000, gives a return of 25 percent, equal to the return of the other assets.) Thus, if the loss on disposal of Equipment A is less than $10,000, segment ROI in the year of disposal is increased. If Equipment A is sold for a $5,000 loss on January 1 (before Equipment A makes any profit contribution), segment ROI still increases from 23.33 percent to 24 percent in the year of disposal, despite the loss of $15,000 profit the equipment would have earned if not disposed of.

SEGMENT X

	Equipment A	All Other Assets
Gross BV	– 0 –	$500,000
Profit before loss	– 0 –	125,000
Disposal loss		(5,000)
Profit after loss		120,000
ROI		24%

In subsequent years, with Equipment A and its contribution to profit gone, the Segment X operating profit is reduced by $15,000 per year, but ROI is increased to 25 percent due to the reduced investment base.

	SEGMENT X
	All Other Assets
Gross BV	$500,000
Profit	125,000
ROI	25%

The effect of valuing the asset base at gross book value is generally dysfunctional. The segment manager would be motivated to dispose of Equipment A even if its 15 percent return was above the cost of capital. The manager would be motivated to dispose of the equipment even if it were fully depreciated and its net book value was zero.

Replacement Decisions.

When assets are replaced, the company must invest an amount equal to the cost of the new asset minus the salvage value of the old asset. But the use of gross book value as the segment's investment value causes its assets to increase by only the difference between the cost of the new asset added to the books and the cost of the old asset removed. To the segment manager, this means that the additional investment to obtain new assets is quite small, and replacement investments can be made (from the segment manager's perspective) at far, far less than the cutoff rate used in cash flow models.

For example, if a manager acquires a new asset for $45,000 to replace one that cost $35,000, the manager may pay $45,000, but the increase in the gross book value of the investment base is only $10,000 (investment base + $45,000 − $35,000 = new investment base). The increase is the same here whether the old asset is relatively new or completely depreciated, because it is the *gross* book value of the old machine that is counted in the investment base.

If segment earnings then increase by $2,000, the additional investment appears to earn a return of $2,000/$10,000, or 20 percent. But if the old asset was only worth $5,000 as a trade-in, the cash investment required is actually $40,000, and the average return only $2,000/ $40,000, or 5 percent.

Net Book Value

Net book value is the value at which an asset is carried in the books (the accounting records). Net book value is original cost minus any cost already depleted, amortized, or depreciated. For instance, a building that cost $500,000 and on which $100,000 in depreciation expense had been taken has a book value of $400,000. Net book value, in companies with one asset or assets of a similar age, gives a decreasing investment base. This effect is increased when accelerated depreciation methods are used. Because the net book value of an asset is less each year, ROI increases each year. This effect misleads segment managers and may cause them to avoid investing in new assets.

Suppose a segment has an investment of $200,000 and net income of $30,000, as follows. ROI is 15 percent ($30,000/$200,000).

Investment:	
Cash	$20,000
Inventory	30,000
Plant and equipment	150,000
Total investment in assets	$200,000
Net income	$30,000
ROI	15%

Calculating ROI for Additional Investments

ROI of the additional investment is calculated based on the out-of-pocket cost of the investment:

Cost of new asset	$45,000
Trade-in (salvage) of old asset	5,000
Cash cost of new asset	$40,000
Increased return	2,000
ROI based on additional investment	5%

ROI of the additional investment is calculated based on the increase in gross book value:

Cost of new asset	$45,000
Cost of old asset	35,000
Increase in gross book value	$10,000
Increased return	2,000
ROI based on increased gross value	20%

This is misleading. The cost to the company of the new asset is $40,000 (as we saw), but valuing the investment base at gross book value obscures this cost at the segment level and encourages the segment manager to make capital budgeting decisions in a foolish (from the company's perspective) way. With gross book value, the objectives of the segment manager are not congruent with the objectives of the company as a whole.

EXHIBIT 3.3

Increasing ROI Using Net Book Value

End of Year	Assets at Cost	Annual Depreciation
1	$200,000	$30,000
2	200,000	30,000
3	200,000	30,000
4	200,000	30,000
5	200,000	30,000

Even if the segment keeps exactly the same assets and earns exactly the same profit each year, ROI will not remain 15 percent because the plant and equipment are depreciated each year. Assume the plant and equipment have a life of five years and that depreciation expense of $30,000 ($150,000/5 years) is taken each year. Depreciation expense is charged against earnings each year and the book value of the investment is reduced to zero over the asset's life.

If cash, inventory, and profit remain the same, the net book value of the segment investment and the ROI calculated on the book value is as shown in Exhibit 3.3. ROI is based on net book value at the end of each year, and increases from 17.6 percent at the end of year one to 60 percent at the end of year five when the plant and equipment are fully depreciated (net book value = zero). The 15 percent ROI occurs only in year one, and only if the net book value of assets at the beginning of the year is used. By the end of the year, the book value has been decreased by the depreciation expense and the ROI has increased.

Accumulated Depreciation to Date	Book Value	Profit	ROI%
$30,000	$170,000	$30,000	17.6
60,000	140,000	30,000	21.4
90,000	110,000	30,000	27.3
120,000	80,000	30,000	37.5
150,000	50,000	30,000	60.0

This effect (increasing ROI) occurs in companies with only one asset or companies that purchase all their assets in the same year. When a company purchases assets in different years, the distortion is still present but averages out and is apparent. Additionally, when ROI is calculated using net book value at the beginning of the year, it is different from ROI calculated using book value at the end of the year. Some companies attempt to overcome this by using the average of beginning and ending book values. In our example, we can calculate the following equally acceptable ROIs for year one.

Using beginning of year book value $30,000/$200,000 ROI = 15.0%
Using end of year book value $30,000/$170,000 ROI = 17.6%
Using average book value for year $30,000/$185,000 ROI = 16.2%

This problem can be avoided by using replacement cost and annuity depreciation. Annuity depreciation uses a mathematical procedure that results in larger depreciation charges as the asset ages. It is cumbersome to apply and produces a pattern of depreciation expense that does not match the way assets wear out. Accountants always mention annuity depreciation when discussing this problem, but we know of no company that uses annuity depreciation.

Replacement Value

Replacement cost is defined several different ways. Assume one segment of a company uses computerized printing equipment that cost $140,000 when purchased five years ago. The equipment has a seven-year life, is depreciated $20,000 per year, and after five years has a net book value of $40,000 [$140,000 − (5 × $20,000)]. Its replacement cost can be estimated using at least four approaches, each leading to a different value.

Replacement Value As Is.

This is the cost of replacing the equipment with used equipment in the same condition. If there is no used equipment market and the equipment to be valued is unique, replacement value can be difficult to estimate. Assume used equipment in the same condition is in demand for use as parts in repairing old processes and costs $60,000 (the amounts in this example are for illustration only).

Replacement Value New.

The cost of replacing the equipment with new equipment of exactly the same model and type is $200,000. Because the equipment is old, new equipment exactly like the old equipment does not exist and requires expensive, custom manufacture. Equipment using computer chips two or three generations old is frequently no longer manufactured.

Capacity Replacement Value.

The cost of replacing not the equipment but the *capacity* of the equipment with equipment currently manufactured is the capacity replacement value. For computerized equipment, new technology often makes it less expensive to purchase the same capacity each year. New equipment that can perform the same work as the old printing equipment costs $90,000.

Price-Level Adjusted Historical Cost.

Although not a true measure of replacement cost, some companies adjust an asset's cost for changes in prices to estimate a current cost. If the price index changed from 110 to 165 during the five years the company has owned the equipment, the price-level adjusted cost of the equipment is $140,000 \times 165/110 = $210,000$.

Even when a definition of replacement cost is chosen, a company may have great difficulty obtaining annual replacement value estimates of the collections of assets that make up the factories, stores, and other operating investments of each segment. Estimates by consultants or appraisers are often subjective and may vary widely.

Economic Value

The economic value is the present value of an asset's future cash flows. It is subjective and difficult to determine. To estimate economic value, managers must both estimate the future cash flows and decide on an appropriate discount rate. These estimated flows must be the flows expected to occur, not the flows managers might target or aspire to.

These expected actual cash flows are then discounted to their present value.

This process produces a conflict between determining the economic value of the investment from predictions of the segment manager's performance, and evaluating the segment manager's performance using the profit generated and the present value of top management's predictions. Performance is, in effect, evaluated against an estimate of itself.

Additionally, the economic value approach gives the same value to an asset, regardless of how it was obtained, wisely or otherwise. If a manager saves on an equipment acquisition by shopping wisely or building the asset in-house, the manager is assigned the same dollar investment base as another manager who acts foolishly and buys identical equipment at a high price (assuming the estimated cash flows and discount rate are the same). Since ROI is supposed to improve a segment management's motivation and top management's evaluation procedures, this is a serious problem.

To illustrate, assume two retail stores in Kansas City are owned by C. C. Smith, who wishes to value the assets of the two store managers using the economic value approach. Coincidentally, Smith decides the stores should begin delivering to customers and directs the managers to purchase one delivery truck each and begin this service as economically as possible. Smith estimates the cash flows from the delivery service will be $10,000 per year, and the trucks will each last five years. Smith believes the appropriate discount rate is 10 percent.

One store manager shops wisely and purchases a new truck with the minimum basic equipment for $24,000. The other manager understands the economic value method and buys a top-of-the-line truck loaded with options for $40,000. What value is placed on each manager's truck? The present value of $10,000 each year for five years at 10 percent is

3.791 × $10,000 = $37,910. Thus, the investment base of each manager is increased by $37,910, the economic value of the truck.

Finally, managers resist the use of economic value. They do not like to be evaluated with artificial measures concocted by economists. As a result, economic value is not often used to value the investment base in ROI measures.

Summary

Managers can use ROI to make decisions about which assets to acquire and which to sell. The decision process involves deciding how to measure return and how to measure the asset base that would be assumed to generate the return. It is important to define these in a way that is appropriate to the evaluation of segment performance versus the evaluation of management performance. Methods for valuing assets include gross book value, net book value, replacement cost, and economic value.

CHAPTER 4

Variations of ROI

After reading this chapter, you will be able to

- Understand the gross margin return on investment (GMROI)
- Understand the components of the GMROI
- Understand the differences between the GMROI and the ROI
- Understand how to improve the GMROI
- Understand the contribution margin return on investment (CMROI)
- Understand the nature of fixed costs and variable costs
- Understand the difference in the contribution margin income statement and the gross profit income statement
- Be able to compare the CMROI and the GMROI to the ROI
- Understand the relationship between cash flow and quality of earnings
- Understand the cash return on investment

Gross Margin Return on Investment (GMROI)

There are several variations of ROI. One is called *gross margin return on investment* (GMROI), and it examines the relationship between the gross margin on sales and the investment in inventory required to support the sales. GMROI is gross margin in dollars for some period divided by the average cost of inventory on hand during the same period.

$$\text{GMROI} = \frac{\textbf{gross margin}}{\textbf{average inventory (at cost)}}$$

The numerator, gross margin, is sales minus the cost of goods (inventory) sold. Sales of $1,000 and cost of goods sold of $600 yield a gross margin of $400. This calculation is often made in the first three lines of the income statement.

Sales	$1,000
Cost of goods sold	600
Gross margin	$ 400

If the $1,000 in sales requires an average inventory equal to two months' cost of sales ($600/12 × 2 months or $100), GMROI is 400 percent, or $4 for every $1 invested in inventory.

$$\text{GMROI} = \frac{\textbf{gross margin}}{\textbf{average inventory (at cost)}} = \frac{\textbf{\$400}}{\textbf{\$100}} = \textbf{400\%}$$

Comparing GMROI and ROI

GMROI differs from ROI in two ways: GMROI uses gross margin instead of net income as the return (gross margin is simply higher up than net income on the income statement), and it considers only the investment in inventory. Since net income is usually small relative to a company's total investment in assets, ROI calculated using a company's net income and total assets is almost always less than 20 percent. But gross margin is substantially larger than net income. And average inventory is generally much smaller than total assets. Because of this, GMROI is often quite large relative to ROI.

Managers believe gross margin and the gross margin percentage are important measures. When managers say, "We make a dollar on each shirt sold," they typically mean, "We sell each shirt for a dollar more than its cost." If a shirt that costs $2 is sold for $3, the gross margin is $1. The gross margin percentage is 33.3 percent, calculated by dividing gross margin by the selling price ($1/$3).

Net income is determined by subtracting cost of goods sold and all other expenses from sales. The net income created on the sale of each shirt might be only $0.20 after the costs of salespeople, supervision, rent, utilities, advertising, and other costs are subtracted from gross margin. Gross margin must be large enough to cover all these other expenses or the company will incur a loss.

Components of GMROI

Like ROI, GMROI can be broken into margin and turnover components. GMROI = Gross margin on sales $\times$ Inventory turnover. The margin component of GMROI is the percentage gross margin on sales. For the example, gross margin on sales is 40 percent.

$$\frac{\text{Gross margin}}{\text{on sales}} = \frac{\text{gross margin}}{\text{sales}} = \frac{\$400}{\$1,000} = 40\%$$

The turnover component is inventory turnover using sales as the numerator. An alternative calculation for inventory turnover uses cost of goods sold as the numerator.

$$\text{Inventory turnover} = \frac{\text{sales}}{\text{inventory}} = \frac{\$1,000}{\$100} = 10 \text{ times}$$

Combining these components shows how they interact to give a GMROI of 400 percent. A change in either component, margin or turnover, changes GMROI.

TIPS & TECHNIQUES

The Margin Information on the Income Statement

The Income Statement has the following basic structure:

  Sales
- Cost of goods sold
= Gross margin
- Other operating expenses
= Operating income
- Nonoperating expenses
= Net income

A margin is calculated by dividing a subtotal (or bottom line) from the income statement, by the top line, Sales. Obviously, a margin has to be less than 100 percent.

GMROI = Gross margin on sales × Inventory turnover

$$\text{GMROI} = \frac{\text{gross margin}}{\text{sales}} \times \frac{\text{sales}}{\text{inventory}}$$

$$\text{GMROI} = \frac{\$400}{\$1,000} \times \frac{\$1,000}{\$100}$$

$$\text{GMROI} = .40 \times 10 = 400\%$$

Improving GMROI

Managers can improve their GMROI by improving either gross margin, inventory turnover, or both. Gross margin can be increased by either increasing selling price to increase the sales dollars generated from a given cost of goods sold, or by reducing the cost of goods sold without reducing sales dollars. Turnover can be increased by reducing average inventory or increasing sales (or both).

Increasing Gross Margin

For retailers, the selling price and the cost of inventory sold are often set by market forces. A retail store must sell at competitive prices and often must buy its inventory from the same sources that supply its competition. Consequently, a retail store that seeks to change its gross margin must negotiate discounts for buying in large quantities or for buying much of its inventory from the same vendor.

Manufacturers have more opportunities to work toward lower costs than do retailers. Manufacturing costs are composed of three components: raw materials, labor, and overhead. Managers can often lower the cost of manufactured inventory by negotiating lower costs on materials, by automating processes to reduce labor, or by adopting one of the newer manufacturing techniques such as using robotics or just-in-time manufacturing.

In our earlier example, GMROI is 400 percent. If management increases selling prices by 10 percent (from $1,000 to $1,100) with no loss in volume, gross margin percentage is increased to .4545 (a repeating decimal), turnover is increased to 11, and GMROI is increased to 500 percent, or $5 for every $1 invested in inventory.

$$\text{GMROI} = \frac{\text{gross margin}}{\text{sales}} \times \frac{\text{sales}}{\text{inventory}}$$

Original performance:

$$\text{GMROI} = \frac{\$400}{\$1,000} \times \frac{\$1,000}{\$100}$$

$$\text{GMROI} = .40 \times 10 = 400\%$$

Improved performance (10% increase in sales dollars):

$$\text{GMROI} = \frac{\$500}{\$1,100} \times \frac{\$1,100}{\$100}$$

$$\text{GMROI} = .4545 \times 11 = 500\%$$

Increasing Turnover

As this example shows, increasing sales to improve gross margin serves a dual purpose because it also increases inventory turnover. Likewise, lower-raw material prices or automated processes reduce the per-unit cost of manufactured inventory, which increases both gross margin per unit and inventory turnover. If managers are able to reduce the cost per unit by 5 percent, both inventory on hand and cost of goods sold are decreased by 5 percent. If sales remains at our original $1,000 level, and cost of goods sold is reduced by 5 percent to $570, gross margin is increased to $430. Gross margin percentage is increased to .43, turnover is increased to 10.53, and GMROI is increased to 453 percent, or $4.53 for every $1 invested in inventory.

	Original performance	5% reduction in unit manufacturing costs
Sales	$1,000	$1,000
Cost of goods sold	600	570
Gross margin	$ 400	$ 430
Inventory	$ 100	$ 95

Improved performance (5% reduction in unit manufacturing costs):

$$\text{GMROI} = \frac{\text{gross margin}}{\text{sales}} \times \frac{\text{sales}}{\text{inventory}}$$

$$\text{GMROI} = \frac{\$430}{\$1,000} \times \frac{\$1,000}{\$95}$$

$$\text{GMROI} = .430 \times 10.53 = 453\%$$

Just-in-time (JIT) and other advanced manufacturing approaches reduce a manufacturer's investment in inventory by reducing both the per-unit manufacturing cost and the time raw materials and partially completed goods are held before being processed. When the length of time inventories are held is reduced, the average investment in inventories is reduced.

To illustrate, our original example assumed cost of goods sold to be $600,000 and an average inventory on hand equal to two months' cost of sales ($600,000/12 = $50,000/month × 2 = $100,000). If JIT and other measures allowed management to reduce inventory between processes to only one-half of one month's cost of sales, ($600,000/12 = $50,000/month × .50 = $25,000), turnover is increased to 40, and GMROI increases to 1600 percent, or $16 for each dollar of investment in inventory.

$$\text{GMROI} = \frac{\text{gross margin}}{\text{sales}} \times \frac{\text{sales}}{\text{inventory}}$$

$$\text{GMROI} = \frac{\$400}{\$1,000} \times \frac{\$1,000}{\$25}$$

$$\text{GMROI} = .40 \times 40 = 1600\%$$

For a competitor who does not adopt a JIT approach to manufacturing, an equivalent GMROI is impossible. Assume a competitor who has not adopted JIT has identical sales and still requires two months' cost of sales to remain in inventory. Turnover is still 10 (as in our original calculation), and to generate a GMROI of 1600 percent, gross margin percentage must be 160 percent, requiring gross margin to be greater than sales! Such a result is impossible.

$$\text{GMROI} = \frac{\text{gross margin}}{\text{sales}} \times \frac{\text{sales}}{\text{inventory}}$$

$$\text{GMROI} = \frac{?}{\$1,000} \times \frac{\$1,000}{\$100}$$

$$\text{GMROI} = 1.60 \times 10 = 1600\%$$

Gross margin percentage must be 160 percent.

Including Markup in GMROI

The analysis of financial ratios is more an art than a science. Therefore, analysts may use different variations of the ratios. Instead of determining inventory turnover with sales as the numerator (as shown previously), we can use cost of goods sold as the numerator and expand the components to include markup. In our original example, markup on cost is 166.7 percent and inventory turnover using cost of goods sold is 6.0.

$$\text{Markup on cost} = \frac{\text{sales}}{\text{cost of goods sold}} = \frac{\$1,000}{\$600} = 166.7\%$$

$$\text{Inventory turnover} = \frac{\text{cost of goods sold}}{\text{inventory}} = \frac{\$600}{\$100} = 6 \text{ times}$$

Combining these new components shows how they interact to explain a GMROI of 400 percent. GMROI is not changed by using these new components, but a change in any component, margin, markup, or turnover changes GMROI.

$$\text{GMROI} = \text{gross margin} \times \text{markup} \times \text{inventory turnover}$$

$$\text{GMROI} = \frac{\text{gross margin}}{\text{sales}} \times \frac{\text{sales}}{\text{cost of goods sold}} \times \frac{\text{cost of goods sold}}{\text{inventory}}$$

$$\text{GMROI} = \frac{\$400}{\$1,000} \times \frac{\$1,000}{\$600} \times \frac{\$600}{\$100}$$

$$\text{GMROI} = .40 \times 1.667 \times 6 = 400\%$$

Markup is the factor that drives gross margin: Higher markups produce higher gross margins. Including markup in the components gives added flexibility to managers trying to increase GMROI. When the relationships are presented in this form, managers see that they can improve GMROI by increasing either gross margin, markup, or inventory turnover.

Types of Costs

When a manufacturer produces more than it sells and thus increases the number of units it keeps in inventory, some costs assigned to the increased inventory are real costs that require additional current expenditures and some are not. Additional electricity is consumed and assembly employees work more hours for which they must be paid. These are real cost increases. Other costs assigned to inventory are not-so-real costs that do not require additional current expenditures. These costs consist either of allocations (assignments) of costs incurred in prior years, such as depreciation on a plant, or costs that would be spent in the same amount even if production had not increased, such as the cost of fire insurance or property taxes.

Fixed Costs

Fixed costs are costs that do not change in total when a company's activity level changes. If depreciation on the factory building is $60,000 per month, it remains $60,000 per month regardless of whether the factory operates one shift or three. If production increases from 10,000 units for one shift to 60,000 units for three, the average depreciation cost per unit decreases from $6 per unit ($60,000/10,000 units), to $1 per unit ($60,000/60,000 units) but total depreciation cost does not change.

Thus, there is no *incremental (or increased) fixed cost* associated with increased activity. Fixed costs for a manufacturer are generally not the costs of production but are instead the costs of maintaining the capacity to produce.

Variable Costs

Variable costs are costs that *do* change in total when a company's activity level changes. Variable costs for a manufacturer include the costs of materials, labor, and some overhead (called direct overhead), such as electricity consumed and the maintenance of equipment. If $20 of raw material

Z is needed to produce one unit of product, the total cost of raw material Z is $200,000 when 10,000 units are produced ($20 × 10,000 units) but $600,000 when 30,000 units are produced ($20 × 30,000 units).

A variable cost is an *incremental (or increased) cost* associated with increased activity. The increased cost of producing an additional order is sometimes called the *marginal cost* of producing the order. In our example, the variable cost per unit for raw materials remains the same ($20), but total costs vary directly with activity. The marginal cost of producing an additional 100 units is $2,000 (100 units × $20).

Contribution Margin Return on Investment (CMROI)

We have discussed the usefulness of gross margin in assessing profitability, but many managers avoid gross margin and use contribution margin instead in their decision making. The contribution margin return on investment (CMROI) is a refinement of the gross margin return on investment (GMROI). CMROI is often more appropriate for assessing performance or making decisions because it recognizes that costs are not all the same. Unlike gross margin, contribution margin is generally not available to persons outside a company.

CMROI examines the relationship between the contribution margin on sales and the incremental investment in inventory required to support the sales. Contribution margin is calculated by subtracting total variable costs from sales. CMROI uses a contribution margin subtotal sometimes called *manufacturing margin* or *manufacturing contribution margin,* calculated by subtracting only variable manufacturing costs (as in variable cost of goods sold) from sales. Variable costs of selling and administration, such as commissions or collections, are then subtracted from manufacturing contribution margin to get contribution margin.

Manufacturing contribution margin and contribution margin are calculated as shown in the contribution margin formatted income state-

---

EXHIBIT 4.1

Contribution Margin and Gross Profit Formatted Income Statements

Bunchy Company Contribution Margin Income Statement for the year ended December 31, 200X

Sales		$500,000
Variable cost of goods sold		150,000
Manufacturing contribution margin		350,000
Variable selling costs	$ 25,000	
Variable administrative costs	50,000	75,000
Contribution margin		275,000
Fixed costs:		
Manufacturing	$150,000	
Selling	37,500	
Administrative	12,500	200,000
Net income		$75,000

Bunchy Company Gross Profit Income Statement for the year ended December 31, 200X

Sales		$500,000
Cost of goods sold		300,000
Gross profit		200,000
Selling costs	$62,500	
Administrative costs	62,500	125,000
Net income		$75,000

---

ment in Exhibit 4.1. Exhibit 4.1 also contains a gross profit formatted or multiple-step income statement. With additions for selling and administrative costs, both income statements contain figures from the main example used throughout the last chapter.

If $500,000 in sales (from Exhibit 4.1) requires an average investment in the variable cost of inventory equal to two months' variable cost of sales ($150,000/12 = $12,500 × 2), or $25,000, CMROI is 1400 percent, or $14 for every $1 invested in the variable cost of inventory.

$$\text{CMROI} = \frac{\text{manufacturing contribution margin}}{\text{average inventory (at variable cost)}} = \frac{\$350,000}{\$25,000} = 1400\%$$

Two-Component CMROI Analysis

Like ROI or GMROI, CMROI can be broken into margin and turnover components. The margin component of CMROI is the manufacturing contribution margin percentage. In our example, manufacturing contribution margin is 70 percent.

$$\text{Manufacturing contribution margin\%} = \frac{\text{manufacturing CM}}{\text{sales}} = \frac{\$350,000}{\$500,000} = 70\%$$

As with GMROI, the turnover component is inventory turnover, but now the variable cost of inventory is the denominator.

$$\text{Inventory turnover} = \frac{\text{sales}}{\text{inventory}} = \frac{\$500,000}{\$25,000} = 20 \text{ times}$$

These components combine to give the CMROI.

$$\text{CMROI} = \frac{\text{manufacturing contribution margin}}{} \times \text{inventory turnover}$$

$$\text{CMROI} = \frac{\text{manufacturing contribution margin}}{\text{sales}} \times \frac{\text{sales}}{\text{inventory variable cost}}$$

$$\text{CMROI} = .70 \times 20 = 1400\%$$

Three-Component CMROI Analysis

As with GMROI, CMROI can be broken into three components if we calculate inventory turnover using the variable cost of sales (rather than sales). The three components generated are margin, markup, and turnover. The margin component of CMROI is the manufacturing contribution margin percentage, as calculated previously. Markup and turnover both use variable cost of goods sold.

$$\text{markup} = \frac{\text{sales}}{\text{variable cost of goods sold}} = \frac{\$500{,}000}{\$150{,}000} = 333.3\%$$

$$\text{Inventory turnover} = \frac{\text{variable cost of goods sold}}{\text{inventory}} = \frac{\$150{,}000}{\$25{,}000} = 6 \text{ times}$$

These three components combine to give the CMROI.

$$\text{CMROI} = \text{manufacturing CM\%} \times \text{markup} \times \text{inventory turnover}$$

$$\text{CMROI} = \frac{\text{manufacturing CM}}{\text{sales}} \times \frac{\text{sales}}{\text{variable cost of goods sold}} \times \frac{\text{variable cost of goods sold}}{\text{inventory}}$$

$$\text{CMROI} = .70 \times 3.333 \times 6 = 1400\%$$

Comparing CMROI and GMROI

The excess of sales over variable cost of goods sold is a better measure of the benefit of selling more inventory than the excess of sales over the full cost of goods sold. Likewise, the variable cost of units placed in inventory is a better measure of the investment required to maintain an inventory. Because fixed costs do not change in total when inventory is increased or decreased, they are usually irrelevant to decisions and should not be in ratios used to evaluate managerial performance.

Because contribution margin affects income so much more directly than gross margin, CMROI is a much more valuable analysis tool than GMROI. Contribution margin can be increased by either increasing selling price or reducing variable costs. Decreasing a bookkeeping allocation of fixed cost to cost of goods sold increases GMROI but does not change

CMROI. Because bookkeeping allocations of fixed costs do not change total costs in any way, it makes sense that CMROI does not change.

Cash Return on Investment

So far we have discussed ROI calculated using net income, gross profit, and manufacturing contribution margin. Now we are going to look at an ROI variation that defines return as cash inflow from operations.

Cash Flow and Quality of Earnings

Operating cash inflow is the most rigorous measure of return on investment that we can take. To stockholders and other investors, income is of high quality only if it is accompanied by an appropriate cash inflow. Income not accompanied by cash inflow is perceived to be of low quality. Low-quality earnings result in a lower market value for a company's stock because analysts believe that earnings accompanied by cash flows are worth more than earnings that are not.

Low quality also results when earnings cannot be sustained or when accounting procedures increase earnings without a corresponding increase in cash flow. High-quality earnings can be sustained and are accompanied by appropriate cash inflows.

Earnings are not accompanied by sustainable cash flows when managers attempt to increase earnings by changing the timing of revenues and expenses. For example, managers might avoid some maintenance procedures to reduce expenses and raise income. If maintenance costing $50,000 is put off until next year, profits this year are improved by $50,000 but earnings next year are reduced by the same amount. Likewise, managers might try to increase sales this year by relaxing credit standards, creating sales that benefit the current year but that are more likely to become bad debts in the following year.

Investors also downgrade the quality of earnings when a company chooses an accounting method because it maximizes reported earnings. Companies that use straight-line depreciation or FIFO inventory are perceived to have lower-quality earnings than a company that uses an accelerated depreciation method or LIFO inventory.[2] (Both straight-line depreciation and FIFO inventory increase reported earnings relative to companies that use an accelerated depreciation method or LIFO inventory.)

Cash ROI

Cash ROI is determined by dividing cash flow from operations during a period by the average investment in total assets during the same period. If average assets are $400,000 and cash from operations is $20,000, cash ROI is 5 percent.

$$\text{Cash ROI} = \frac{\text{cash flow from operations}}{\text{average total assets}} = \frac{\$20,000}{\$400,000} = .05$$

Like other variations of ROI, cash ROI can be divided into a return on sales component and a turnover component. The return on sales component is cash return on sales, and the turnover is the turnover of total investment in assets. If sales are $500,000, cash return on sales is 4 percent and asset turnover is 1.5.

$$\text{Cash ROI} = \text{cash return on sales} \times \text{asset turnover}$$

$$\text{Cash ROI} = \frac{\text{cash flow from operations}}{\text{sales}} \times \frac{\text{sales}}{\text{average assets}}$$

$$\text{Cash ROI} = \frac{\$20,000}{\$500,000} \times \frac{\$500,000}{\$400,000}$$

$$\text{Cash ROI} = .04 \times 1.25 = .05$$

Cash return on sales is a cash flow ratio similar to the *profitability ratio,* return on sales (i.e., net income/sales). Cash return on sales helps investors evaluate the quality of a company's earnings and determine the extent it can support its net income with cash flow.

The asset turnover ratio measures management's effectiveness in using the company's total assets to generate sales activity.

Estimating Cash Flow from Operations

Cash flow from operations is shown in every published cash flow statement. Still, it is common for people to estimate it from net income by adding depreciation and amortization expense to net income. Cash is consumed when a company purchases an asset such as a plant or a patent, but no cash flow occurs when the cost of the asset is depreciated or amortized against earnings each year. Depreciation and amortization expenses are allocations of an asset's original cost to a period benefited by the asset's use. Because of this, depreciation and amortization are operating expenses that do not require operating cash outflows each year.

Because these two operating expenses subtracted in the income statement do not require cash outflows, many people think that adding them back to net income gives a good approximation of cash from operations. Exhibits 4.2 and 4.3 show the 2000 income statement for Bristol-Myers Squibb Company. We estimate cash from operations by adding Bristol-Myers depreciation of $746,000,000 to its net income of $4,711,000,000. Bristol-Myers's cash flow from operations is estimated to be $5,457,000,000. In Exhibit 4.4 Bristol-Myers's statement of cash flows shows net cash from operating activities as $4,652,000,000.

The statement of cash flows published in a company's annual report shows cash flow, in or out, for three separate activities: operating, financing, and investing. Two methods may be used in the statement of cash flows to determine and present cash flow from operating activities: the direct method and the indirect method.

EXHIBIT 4.2

Income Statement for Bristol–Myers Squibb Company

	Fiscal Year		
	2000	**1999**	**1998**
Net sales	$18,216	$16,878	$15,061
Expenses:			
Cost of products sold	4,759	4,542	3,896
Marketing, selling and administrative	3,860	3,789	3,685
Advertising and product promotion	1,672	1,549	1,518
Research and development	1,939	1,759	1,506
Special charge	—	—	800
Provision for restructuring	508	—	157
Gain on sale of business	(160)	—	(201)
Other	160	81	62
	12,738	11,720	11,423
Earnings from continuing operations before income taxes	5,478	5,158	3,638
Provision for income taxes	1,382	1,369	888
Earnings from continuing operations	4,096	3,789	2,750
Discontinued operations			
Net earnings	375	378	391
Net gain on disposal	240	—	—
	615	378	391
Net earnings	$4,711	$4,167	$3,141
Earnings per common share			
Basic			
Earnings from continuing operations	$2.08	$1.91	$1.38
Discontinued operations			
Net earnings	.19	.19	.20

EXHIBIT 4.2

INCOME STATEMENT FOR BRISTOL-MYERS CONTINUED

	Fiscal Year		
	2000	**1999**	**1998**
Net gain on disposal	.13	—	—
	.32	.19	.20
Net earnings	$2.40	$2.10	$1.58
Diluted			
Earnings from continuing operations	$2.05	$1.87	$1.36
Discontinued operations	.19	.19	.19
Net gain on disposal	.12	—	—
	.31	.19	.19

The Direct Method.

The direct method is essentially a cash basis income statement. Operating cash flows are separated into major categories of receipts and payments and their net amount is the cash flow provided by or used in operations. There is no cash flow for depreciation or amortization, so these expenses are not used in determining cash flow from operations using the direct method. Likewise, the amount of a gain or loss shown in an income statement does not show the amount or direction of any related cash flow. Land with a cost of $9,000 that is sold for $7,000 produces a loss of $2,000 but a cash inflow of $7,000. Because a sale of land is not an operating activity, the $7,000 inflow would appear as an investing activity cash inflow, a separate category appearing below cash from operations in a statement of cash flows.

We see the general form of the direct method in Exhibit 4.5.

The Indirect Method.

The indirect method of preparing and presenting cash flow adjusts net income up or down for differences between revenues and expenses and the actual cash flows from operations. Differences between the income

EXHIBIT 4.3

Balance Sheet for Bristol-Myers Squibb Company

Bristol-Myers Squibb Company Consolidated Balance Sheet

	December 31,		
Dollars in Millions	**2000**	**1999**	**1998**
Assets			
Current Assets:			
Cash and cash equivalents	$3,182	$2,720	$2,244
Time deposits and marketable securities	203	237	285
Receivables, net of allowances	3,662	3,272	3,190
Inventories	1,831	2,126	1,873
Prepaid expenses	946	912	1,190
Total Current Assets	9,824	9,267	8,782
Property, plant and equipment	4,548	4,621	4,429
Insurance recoverable	262	468	523
Excess of cost over net tangible assets arising from business acquisitions	1,436	1,502	1,587
Other Assets	1,508	1,256	951
Total Assets	$17,578	$17,114	$16,272
Liabilites			
Current Liabilities:			
Short-term borrowings	$162	$432	$482
Accounts payable	1,702	1,657	1,380
Accrued expenses	2,881	2,367	2,302
Product liability	186	287	877
U.S. and foreign income taxes payable	701	794	750
Total Current Liabilities	5,632	5,537	5,791

EXHIBIT 4.3

BALANCE SHEET FOR BRISTOL-MYERS CONTINUED

	December 31,		
Dollars in Millions	**2000**	**1999**	**1998**
Other Liabilities	1,430	1,590	1,541
Long-Term debt	1,336	1,342	1,364
Total Liabilities	8,398	8,469	8,696
Stockholders' Equity			
Preferred stock, $2 convertible series: Authorized 10 million shares; issued and outstanding 9,864 in 2000, 10,977 in 1999, and 11,684 in 1998, liquidation value of $50 per share	—	—	—
Common stock, par value of $.10 per share: Authorized 4.5 billion shares; 2,197,900,835 issued in 2000, 2,192,970,504 in 1999, and 2,188,316,808 in 1998	220	219	219
Capital in excess of par value of stock	2,002	1,533	1,075
Other comprehensive income	(1,103)	(816)	(622)
Retained earnings	17,781	15,000	12,540
	18,900	15,936	13,212
Less cost of treasury stock—244,365,726 common shares in 2000, 212,164,851 in 1999, and 199,550,532 in 1998	9,720	7,291	5,636
Total Stockholders' Equity	9,180	8,645	7,576
Total Liabilities and Stockholders' Equity	$17,578	$17,114	$16,272

EXHIBIT 4.4

Statement of Cash Flows for Bristol-Myers Squibb Company

Bristol-Myers Squibb Company Consolidated Statement of Cash Flows

In Millions	Year Ended December 31,		
	2000	1999	1998
Cash Flow From Operating Activities:			
Net earnings	$4,711	$4,167	$3,141
Depreciation and amortization	746	678	625
Special charge	—	—	800
Provision for restructuring/other	542	—	201
Gain from sales of businesses/ product divestitures	(562)	—	(201)
Other operating items	10	(79)	(1)
Receivables	(494)	(176)	(253)
Inventories	75	(317)	(139)
Accounts payable and accrued expenses	256	258	284
Income taxes	(54)	477	34
Product liability	(173)	(726)	(715)
Insurance recoverable	100	59	196
Pension contribution	(230)	—	—
Other assets and liabilities	(275)	(117)	(190)
Net Cash Provided by Operating Activities	4,652	4,224	3,782
Cash Flows From Investing Activities:			
Proceeds from sales of time deposits and marketable securities	45	51	309
Purchases of time deposits and marketable securities	(10)	(4)	(256)
Additions to fixed assets	(589)	(709)	(788)

EXHIBIT 4.4

STATEMENT OF CASH FLOWS FOR BRISTOL-MYERS CONTINUED

	Year Ended December 31,		
In Millions	**2000**	**1999**	**1998**
Proceeds from sales of businesses/product divestitures	848	134	417
Business acquisitions (including purchase of trademarks/patents)	(196)	(266)	(93)
Other, net	(82)	35	65
Net Cash Provided by (Used in) Investing Activities	16	(759)	(346)
Cash Flows From Financing Activities:			
Short-term borrowings	(247)	(26)	(81)
Long-term debt	6	(54)	73
Issuances of common stock under stock plans	352	254	478
Purchases of treasury stock	(2,338)	(1,419)	(1,561)
Dividends paid	(1,930)	(1,707)	(1,551)
Net Cash Used in Financing Activities	(4,157)	(2,952)	(2,642)
Effect of Exchange Rates on Cash	(49)	(37)	(6)
Increase in Cash and Cash Equivalents	462	476	788
Cash and Cash Equivalents at Beginning of Year	2,720	2,244	1,456
Cash and Cash Equivalents at End of Year	$3,182	$2,720	$2,244

The accompanying notes are an Integral part of these financial statements.

statement amounts and the related operating cash flows result in changes in the current asset and liability accounts because, for the most part, each of these accounts is linked directly to an operating revenue or expense. (Inventory and accounts payable, for example, are linked to cost of goods

IN THE REAL WORLD

Cash Flow Analysis for Bristol–Myers Squibb

		2000	1999	1998
Cash ROI =	cash flow from operations / total assets	26.46%	24.68%	23.24%
Cash ROI =	estimated cash flow / total assets	31.04%	28.31%	23.14%
Cash Return on Sales =	cash flow / sales	25.54%	25.03%	25.11%

Cash return on sales demonstrates the most consistent results.

sold, accounts receivable to sales revenue.) Cash provided by operations is thus calculated by (1) adding to net income any changes in current asset or liability accounts that result in increases in cash from operations, and (2) subtracting from net income any changes that result in decreases. Changes in the current accounts affect cash flow, as shown in the following:

Change in Account	Effect on cash from operations	Add (Subtract) to (from) Net Income (NI) to Determine Cash from Operations
Increase in current asset	Decrease in cash	Subtract from NI
Decrease in current asset	Increase in cash	Add to NI
Increase in current liability	Increase in cash	Add to NI
Decrease in current liability	Decrease in cash	Subtract from NI

EXHIBIT 4.5

Operating Cash Flows Using the Direct Method

Caesar Company Schedule of Operating Cash Flows (Direct Method)
for the year ended December 31, 2001

Cash collected from customers		$25,000
Less cash paid for expenses:		
For goods sold	$10,000	
For salaries and wages	7,500	
For other operating costs	5,000	22,500
Net cash provided by operating activities		$ 2,500

Again, because depreciation and amortization expenses do not affect cash flows, they are added back to net income. For the same reason, any losses (or gains) are also adjustments added to (or subtracted from) net income.

Exhibit 4.6 shows the format for the indirect method of determining cash flow from operations for ABC Company. The Bristol-Myers's Statement of Cash Flows in Exhibit 4.4 uses the indirect method to calculate cash from operations.

Summary

The basic, traditional ROI defines return as net income or income from operations. Other variations involve defining the return as the gross margin on sales (gross margin = sales − cost of sales) or as the contribution margin (CM = sales − variable costs) or as the cash flow. The GMROI is gross margin divided by the average cost of inventory (a more limited version of investment than total assets). The CMROI is contribution margin divided by the additional investment in inventory required to support the sales. The cash ROI divides cash flow from

EXHIBIT 4.6

Operating Cash Flows Using the Indirect Method

Caesar Company Schedule of Operating Cash Flows (Indirect Method)
for the year ended December 31, 2001

Net income for 2001		$ 500
Plus:		
Depreciation	$1,500	
Loss on sale of equipment	500	
Increase in wages payable	1,000	
Decrease in accounts receivable	500	3,500
Less:		
Increase in inventory	1,000	
Decrease in accounts payable	500	(1,500)
Net cash provided by operating activities		$ 2,500

operations by total assets. Each ROI version can be broken down into a return on sales and a turnover of some type, either inventory turnover or total asset turnover. As usual, increasing either of the components will result in an improved ROI.

CHAPTER 5

Analyzing Sales Revenues, Costs, and Profits

After reading this chapter, you will be able to

- Understand how to analyze sales revenues
- Understand the effect of the market on sales revenue performance
- Understand the effect of market variance, market share variance, and sales price variance on sales
- Understand the impact of market variance, market share variance, sales price variance, and collection variance on profit
- Understand price and quantity variances
- Understand the cost behavior of variable and fixed costs
- Understand budget variances

Business centers can often be defined by what their managers are responsible for controlling. For example, a revenue center manager controls only sales or some other revenue-generating activity and is not responsible for either the costs incurred or the investment base used. Profit center managers are responsible for maximizing profits (and can control revenues and costs) but not for managing the asset base. An investment center manager controls either a whole company or a segment of a company that operates as an autonomous unit, having both profits and an underlying asset investment base.

Investment, profit, and revenue-center managers contribute to the profitability of a company and to ROI by increasing revenue production as part or all of their duties. Analyzing revenue production involves more than simply looking at the total dollars of revenue generated. It is useful to also analyze changes in the market, variations from budget for total revenues, and any changes from budget in the percentage of customer accounts collected. Such changes and variations need to be considered in the process of variance analysis, which examines differences in actual results and expected results.

Market Size Variance

Managers are aware that the economy in general can have a great impact on what they are trying to achieve. If the market for the company's products changes, sales revenue will change, independent of the performance by a revenue or profit center manager. Any analysis of revenue generation where a company has a substantial market share (perhaps 10 percent or more) should include a determination of the effect of changes in market size.

For example, assume the manager of wholesale refrigerator sales in Chicago is responsible only for the total refrigerator sales revenues generated. The home office is responsible for all facilities, advertising, and other costs. In preparing sales forecasts for the year, the manager establishes a target for Chicago of 50,000 refrigerators at a standard price of $300 each. The revenue center manager actually sells only 40,000 refrigerators during the year, creating a 10,000 unit variance. At the standard selling price, this creates a $3,000,000 unfavorable (UF) variance from forecasted sales.

Forecasted sales	50,000	refrigerators
Actual sales	(40,000)	refrigerators
Variance	10,000	refrigerators UF
	× $300	standard price/refrigerator
	$3,000,000	UF

But to analyze the manager's performance in a meaningful way, we must first look at the expected market for refrigerators in Chicago and the market that actually existed.

Forecasted market	500,000	refrigerators
Actual market	(450,000)	refrigerators
Market variance	50,000	refrigerators UF

From this we see that another way to view the manager's forecast is not as 50,000 refrigerators, but as sales of 10 percent of the Chicago refrigerator market (.10 × 500,000 refrigerators = 50,000 refrigerators). Viewed this way, we see that 5,000 units, or $1,500,000 (5,000 refrigerators × $300 standard price) of the manager's unfavorable variance is due to environmental influences the manager could not control, as follows:

	Market		**Sales @ 10% of Market**	
Forecast	500,000		50,000	refrigerators
Market variance	(50,000)	UF	(5,000)	refrigerators UF
Actual market	450,000			refrigerators
Adjusted forecast			45,000	refrigerators

We must evaluate the manager's performance in relation to the total revenue available. A decline in the size of the refrigerator market is beyond the sales manager's control.

Market Share Variance

Once we have corrected for a variance in the size of the market and its effect on the manager's forecast, we can determine if the manager achieved the target or forecasted market share. Here, the manager expected to sell 45,000 refrigerators (the adjusted target) but sold only 40,000. The manager's market share has declined by 1.22 percent, resulting in an unfavorable variance (UF).

Forecasted market share	50,000/500,000 refrigerators =	10.00%
Less actual market share	40,000/450,000 refrigerators =	8.88%
Market share variance	=	1.12% UF

In units and dollars, the market variance and market share variance are shown as follows.

	Market	**Sales @ 10% of Market**	
Forecast sales	500,000	50,000	refrigerators
Market variance	(50,000)	(5,000)	refrigerators UF
Actual market	450,000	45,000	refrigerators
Actual sales		(40,000)	refrigerators
Market share variance		5,000	refrigerators UF
		× $300	standard price/refrigerator
		$1,500,000	UF

	In Units		**At Standard Price**
	Market	**Sales @ 10% of Market**	**Sales@ $300 Standard/Unit**
Forecast sales	500,000	50,000	$15,000,000
Market variance	(50,000) UF	(5,000) UF	(1,500,000) UF
Actual market	450,000		
Adjusted forecast		45,000	13,500,000
Actual quantity sold		(40,000)	(12,000,000)
Market share variance		5,000 UF	$1,500,000 UF

A manager should be held responsible only for the variance(s) under his or her control. The difference between the manager's forecasted or target sales quantity and actual sales quantity is summarized as follows.

	Units	Sales Dollars @ Standard Price
Forecast sales	50,000	$15,000,000
Market variance	(5,000) UF	(1,500,000) UF
Market share variance	(5,000) UF	(1,500,000) UF
Actual quantity sold at standard prices	40,000	$12,000,000

Sales Volume Variances and Profits

When managers increase or decrease sales revenue by changing the number of units sold, there is also a corresponding change in the cost of goods sold and perhaps other expenses, such as commissions or product delivery costs. Other expenses, like rent or insurance, do not change. Thus, revenues change in direct proportion to a change in units (halving the units sold halves the revenue), but total expenses, and hence profits, do not change in direct proportion to a change in units. Because of this, differences between actual and budgeted sales that result from volume differences, rather than selling price differences, are often stated in terms of their effect on profits.

If our refrigerator with a standard selling price of $300 has a budgeted cost of $200, the effect on budgeted profits of each unit change in sales volume is actually $300 minus $200, or $100, the amount each unit contributes to profit. For simplicity, assume all the costs that change as a result of changes in sales activity (the cost of units, bad debts, commissions, advertising) are contained in the $200 budgeted cost per unit, here called "Cost of sales and other." Assume further that all costs that don't change as a result of changes in sales (rent, insurance) are contained in the $1,500,000 "Other expenses" category. With these assumptions, the company budgets profit of $3,500,000 for the Chicago area.

Budgeted Income for Chicago at Budgeted Quantity

Sales at standard cost (50,000 × $300)	$15,000,000
Cost of sales and other at budgeted cost (50,000 × $200)	10,000,000
Budgeted gross margin	5,000,000
Other expenses not changing with sales	1,500,000
Budgeted net income	$3,500,000

If we change the budgeted sales quantity to the actual sales quantity of 40,000 units, and keep the standard selling price at $300, the budgeted cost per unit at $200, and "Other expenses" at $1,500,000, we find income decreases by $1,000,000. (This is what we expect because we know that each unit sold is budgeted to contribute $100 to profit and 50,000 − 40,000 = 10,000 units × $100 = $1,000,000.)

Budgeted Income for Chicago at Actual Quantity

Sales at standard cost (40,000 × $300)	$12,000,000
Cost of sales and other at budgeted cost (40,000 × $200)	8,000,000
Budgeted gross margin	4,000,000
Other expenses not changing with sales	1,500,000
Budgeted net income at actual quantity	$ 2,500,000

Working from these income statements, our analysis of volume changes due to market and market share variances explain the change in profit, as follows.

	Units	Profit per Unit	Total Profit in Dollars
Forecast profit			$3,500,000
Market variance	(5,000) UF	× $100	(500,000) UF
Market share variance	(5,000) UF	× $100	(500,000) UF
Profit after market variances			$2,500,000

Sales Price Variances

Managers can try to improve the bottom line by increasing market share (as just discussed) or by increasing selling prices. When there is a change in the selling price of a company's products, the increase or decrease goes directly to the bottom line because there is no accompanying change in cost. If the manager in our example actually sold 40,000 refrigerators at $315 (rather than at the forecasted price of $300), the $15 increase in selling price per unit results in a $15 per unit increase in profit. The variance due to the change in selling price is $600,000 favorable (F), as follows.

40,000 units × $15/unit increase in selling price = $600,000 F

At an actual selling price of $315/unit and an actual volume of 40,000 units, total sales revenues are $12,600,000 (40,000 units × $315), and the difference between the manager's forecasted sales and actual sales performance is now summarized as follows. Notice that each of the variances is shown separately to highlight how it alone affects sales, and actual sales contains the effect of all three variances.

	Units	Standard Price per Unit	Sales Dollars
Forecast sales	50,000	× $300	$15,000,000
Sales volume variances:			
Market variance	(5,000) UF	× 300	(1,500,000) UF
Market share variance	(5,000) UF	× 300	(1,500,000) UF
Sales price variance	NA		600,000 F
Actual sales	40,000		$12,600,000

When the actual selling price is $315/unit, the effect on budgeted profits of the market, market share, and sales price variances is shown as follows.

	Units	Standard Profit per Unit	Profit in Dollars
Forecast profit	NA		$3,500,000
Sales volume variances:			
Market variance	(5,000) UF	× $100	(500,000) UF
Market share variance	(5,000) UF	× 100	(500,000) UF
Sales price variance	NA		600,000 F
Actual profit			$3,100,000

Sales Collection Variance

Chapter 4 discusses Cash ROI and points out that earnings must be accompanied by cash flows for investors to believe earnings are of high quality. Cash flows from sales are often determined by the company's ability to collect credit sales. If the company fails to screen customers properly or to anticipate economic downturns, sales result in uncollectible accounts expense rather than in cash inflows.

Thus, it is useful to reconcile budgeted cash collections from sales to actual cash collected from sales. If collection is a problem, determining and isolating a sales collection variance demonstrates that collections are as important as sales volume or selling price.

Assume the company in our example sells on credit and budgets uncollectible sales at 6 percent of total sales. Due to a change in credit policy, the company actually has uncollectible sales of 10 percent. Uncollectible sales are four percentage points (10% − 6%) higher than forecasted, and the sales collection variance is 4 percent of $12,600,000, or $504,000 UF.

An analysis of the difference between actual and budgeted performance that includes a consideration of the cash collection variance follows.

	Units	Sales Dollars
Forecast sales	50,000	$15,000,000
Sales volume variances:		
Market variance	(5,000) UF	(1,500,000) UF
Market share variance	(5,000) UF	(1,500,000) UF
Sales price variance	NA	600,000 F
Actual sales	40,000	$12,600,000
Less:		
Budgeted uncollectible sales (6%)		(756,000)
Budgeted cash collections from sales		$11,844,000
Collection variance (4%)		(504,000) UF
Actual cash collected from sales (90%)		$11,340,000

The company's forecasted profit includes the budgeted uncollectible accounts expense. The collection variance is in substance a variance in uncollectible accounts expense. Changes in uncollectible accounts expense (labeled "Collection variance") are included in a reconciliation of budgeted and actual profits, as follows.

	Units	Profit in Dollars
Forecast profit		$3,500,000
Sales volume variances:		
Market variance	(5,000) UF	(500,000) UF
Market share variance	(5,000) UF	(500,000) UF
Sales price variance		600,000 F
Actual profit before collection variance		$3,100,000
Collection variance		(504,000) UF
Actual profit		$2,596,000

Summary Analysis

The manager in our example forecast sales of 10 percent of the Chicago refrigerator market, to consist of 50,000 refrigerators sold for an average (standard) price of $300 each, or total sales of $15,000,000. The manager's actual profit for the year is $2,596,000 on sales of $12,600,000. Profits are $904,000 less than target, and sales are off by $2,400,000 ($1,500,000 + $1,500,000 − $600,000, or market variance + market share variance − sales price variance).

The manager's performance is analyzed as follows: The Chicago market was 10 percent less than the forecast, and the manager lost 10 percent of the company's predicted unit market share. The combined effect of these losses reduced sales by $3,000,000 and profits by $1,000,000. In response to slow profit growth, the manager increased selling price to average $315 per unit for the year and loosened credit terms. Some of the lost sales dollars were recovered as a result of the increased price. Profits increased by $600,000 as a result of the price change, but fell $504,000 because of higher uncollectibles resulting from the new credit policies.

There may also be variances from the budgeted $200 per unit or the budgeted $1,500,000 in other expenses, but the Chicago manager is responsible only for sales revenues. Some other manager is responsible for any other variances.

Income Performance for Chicago
(With budgeted cost of sales and other expenses but actual quantity,
price, and collection rate controllable by the Chicago manager)

Sales	(40,000 × $315)	$12,600,000
Cost of sales and other at budgeted cost	(40,000 × $200)	8,000,000
Budgeted gross margin		4,600,000
Additional uncollectible accounts expense[*]		504,000
Other expenses not changing with sales (budgeted)		1,500,000
Net income		$ 2,596,000

[*]Because of our beginning assumptions, the budgeted 6 percent uncollectible accounts expense must be included in the $200/unit "Cost of sales and other." Only the 4 percent additional amount is shown as additional uncollectible accounts expense.

Variable Costs Variance

So far we have looked at techniques used to analyze variances in return caused by revenues that vary from a targeted or budgeted level. The remainder of the chapter discusses variances in return resulting from *costs* that are different from budget. The variances in this chapter are used as the starting point in detailed analysis of variations in profit and ROI.

Variable costs are expected to vary in total in direct proportion with activity. Examples of items that are generally variable costs include the cost of energy, raw materials, supplies, maintenance, and assembly-line labor.

Exhibit 5.1 shows the graph of a typical variable cost.

Variable Cost Standards

Variable cost budgets for departments or projects are generally prepared by first estimating the cost of each individual component activity of the department or project. For example, budgets for the cost of the payroll department may begin with budgets for such items as the cost of authorizing and printing one check, or the marginal (or additional) cost of typing and mailing one letter. Total budgeted payroll department costs, then, are determined as the total of 52 weekly payrolls of 200 checks at $150 per check, plus 50,000 letters per year at a budgeted cost per letter of $4, plus budgeted amounts for the costs of other activities.

The cost of each activity for which costs are budgeted separately is often called a *standard cost*. Thus, we speak of the standard cost of printing a weekly payroll check, or the standard cost per letter typed and mailed. Whatever the activity, its total standard cost is determined from the standard or budgeted quantity of an input allowed for a unit and the standard or budgeted cost of the input.

$$\text{standard quantity} \atop \text{of inputs} \times \text{standard price} \atop \text{of inputs} = \text{standard cost} \atop \text{of output}$$

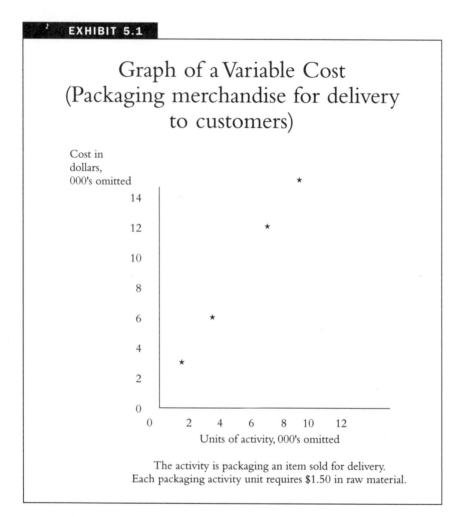

EXHIBIT 5.1

Graph of a Variable Cost
(Packaging merchandise for delivery to customers)

The activity is packaging an item sold for delivery.
Each packaging activity unit requires $1.50 in raw material.

Variances from Budgeted Cost

Mathematically, there are only two things that can cause a variance between the budgeted or standard variable cost and the actual cost incurred: (1) a difference between budgeted *quantity* (such as payrolls or letters typed) and actual quantity of inputs, or (2) a difference between standard and actual *cost* of the inputs. Consider, for example, the standard for letters typed and mailed.

$$\begin{array}{ccc} \text{Budgeted Quantity} & \times & \text{Standard Price} & = & \text{Budgeted Cost} \\ \text{of Inputs} & & \text{of Inputs} & & \text{of Output} \end{array}$$

$$\text{50,000 letters} \quad \times \quad \text{\$4/letter} \quad = \quad \text{\$200,000}$$

The actual, total cost is different from budget if a different quantity of letters are typed, say 55,000 letters instead of the 50,000 budgeted.

$$\begin{array}{ccc} \text{Actual Quantity} & \times & \text{Standard Price} & = & \text{Standard Cost} \\ \text{of Inputs} & & \text{of Inputs} & & \text{of Actual Output} \end{array}$$

$$\text{55,000 letters} \times \quad \text{\$4/letter} \quad = \quad \text{\$220,000}$$

The *quantity variance* is \$20,000 unfavorable (\$220,000 − \$200,000). An alternate way to calculate a quantity variance is

$$\begin{array}{ccc} \text{Change in Quantity} & \times & \text{Standard Price} & = & \text{Quantity} \\ \text{of Inputs} & & \text{of Inputs} & & \text{Variance} \end{array}$$

$$\begin{array}{ccc} \text{5,000 additional} & \times & \text{\$4/letter} & = & \text{\$20,000} \\ \text{letters} & & & & \text{unfavorable} \end{array}$$

Actual results also differ from budget if the activity actually costs more or less than the cost allowed by the standard. Assume the administration department not only types 5,000 more letters than expected, but also pays \$5 per letter typed, rather than the \$4 price budgeted as standard.

$$\begin{array}{ccc} \text{Actual Quantity} & \times & \text{Actual Price} & = & \text{Actual Cost} \\ \text{of Inputs} & & \text{of Inputs} & & \text{of Actual Output} \end{array}$$

$$\begin{array}{ccc} \text{55,000 letters} & \times & \text{\$5/letter} & = & \text{\$275,000} \\ \text{typed} & & & & \end{array}$$

The *price variance* is \$55,000 unfavorable (\$275,000 − \$220,000). An alternate way to calculate a price variance is as follows.

$$\begin{array}{ccc} \text{Actual Quantity} & \times & \text{Change in Price} & = & \text{Price Variance} \\ \text{of Inputs} & & \text{of Inputs} & & \end{array}$$

$$\text{55,000 letters} \times \text{\$1/letter unfavorable} = \text{\$55,000 unfavorable}$$

When 55,000 letters are typed at an actual cost of $5/letter, the total variance is $75,000 unfavorable, analyzed as follows.

The price variance is $55,000 unfavorable.

The quantity variance is <u>$20,000</u> unfavorable.

The total variance is $75,000 unfavorable.

Same Variances, Different Names

Although price and quantity variances for all variable costs are calculated in the same manner, they are often called by different names. Price variances are sometimes called *rate variances* or *spending variances.* Quantity variances are sometimes called *efficiency variances* or *usage variances.* The following are examples of general usage:

- A difference in the hourly wage of an assembly line worker is a *labor rate variance.*

- A difference in the cost of supplies is a *spending variance.*

- A difference in the number of labor hours worked is a *labor efficiency variance.*

- A difference in the quantity of raw materials used is a *materials usage variance.*

When standards are set at realistic levels, favorable variances signal that operations are efficient and effective. Unfavorable variances indicate that operations are inefficient and ineffective. Favorable cost variances result in lower costs and increased net income; unfavorable variances increase costs and reduce net income.

Investigating Causes of Price and Quantity Variances

Separating a variance into its price and quantity components does not tell a manager why the variance occurred. Once managers calculate

TIPS & TECHNIQUES

Many accountants first learned about basic price and quantity variances by using a three-column approach. The first column is made up of only actual information while the third column is made up of only standards. The middle column is a revision of the first in a way that produces the price variance as the difference between the first and middle columns.

Materials Variances (assuming all materials purchased were used):

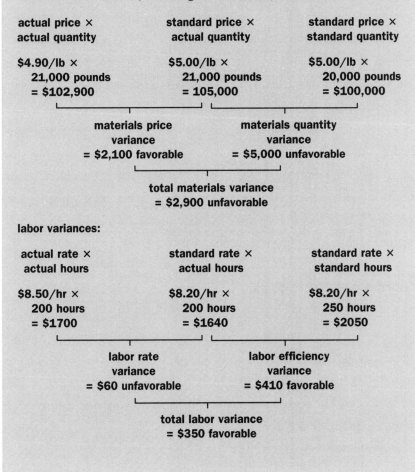

actual price ×
actual quantity

standard price ×
actual quantity

standard price ×
standard quantity

$4.90/lb ×
21,000 pounds
= $102,900

$5.00/lb ×
21,000 pounds
= 105,000

$5.00/lb ×
20,000 pounds
= $100,000

materials price
variance
= $2,100 favorable

materials quantity
variance
= $5,000 unfavorable

total materials variance
= $2,900 unfavorable

labor variances:

actual rate ×
actual hours

standard rate ×
actual hours

standard rate ×
standard hours

$8.50/hr ×
200 hours
= $1700

$8.20/hr ×
200 hours
= $1640

$8.20/hr ×
250 hours
= $2050

labor rate
variance
= $60 unfavorable

labor efficiency
variance
= $410 favorable

total labor variance
= $350 favorable

price and quantity variances, they must investigate to see why the variances occurred. In our example, the actual cost per letter might increase because of a change in the cost of paper or postage. It might simply be that the $4 standard is inaccurate or out of date. The number of letters might increase because the number of employees, customers, or vendors with whom the company corresponds increased. Or perhaps management decided to improve relations by increasing its communications with one of these groups.

Alternately, an increase in computerization or the use of form letters might reduce the cost per letter. Increased use of electronic mail (e-mail) might reduce the number of letters. Exhibit 5.2 lists a few of the causes a manager might find for variances in correspondence cost.

Sometimes a variance in one department is caused by poor work done in another department. If, for instance, an employee in the purchasing department buys low-quality envelopes at a price below the purchasing standard, that will generate a favorable price variance in the purchasing department. But if the envelopes have a poor-quality glue, they might stick together or fail to seal. Difficulty using the cheap, low-quality envelopes might increase the cost to process each letter.

Fixed Cost Variances

Fixed costs are costs that do not vary in total with changes in activity. A fixed cost remains constant or *fixed* in total, despite changes in operating activity. Examples of fixed costs include the cost of fire insurance or property taxes on a building, the lease payment for a computer or car, and the monthly compensation of all salaried workers. Exhibit 5.3 shows the graph of a typical fixed cost.

It is relatively easy to estimate the amount of variable cost per unit of activity: simply increase activity 10 (or 100 or 1,000) units, and total variable costs increase by 10 (or 100 or 1,000) times the variable cost per

EXHIBIT 5.2

Payroll Department:
Reasons for Cost Variances
Processing Correspondence

<u>Price variances may result from:</u>

Changes in postage

Changes in the cost of stationery or envelopes

Changes in the specified quality of stationery or envelopes

Changes in the wages of typists or other workers involved

Changes in the level of skill specified in typist or other job
descriptions

Turnover in the department

Hiring part-time help

Changes in the level of computerization

Aging of equipment

<u>Quantity variances may result from:</u>

Changes in the number of employees or others receiving
correspondence

Increased use of E-mail

Changes in policy

Changes in the use of bulletin boards

Changes in the company environment requiring communication to workers

New management styles

Employee Participation in Variance Analysis

As mentioned in the text, managers must investigate to see why variances occurred. Employees may be in a position to help in this investigation as it relates to efficiency variances, since employees are the ones using the materials to produce a product and spending the labor time on the product. Furthermore, managers often find that when they involve employees in decision making, morale improves and operations become more effective and efficient. According to "America's Elite Factories" in *Fortune* magazine, the Kenworth Truck Plant in Renton, Washington, has experienced this very situation. Employees of Kenworth are encouraged to make suggestions on how to improve efficiency, and the company readily approves good suggestions, recently rearranging placement of parts to economize on employee time spent obtaining parts during production. In the same article, Aeroquip Group in Van Wert, Ohio, is praised for building—and rebuilding—production cells in its quest for greater efficiency and for attaining 95 percent employee participation in its "improvement teams." This participation has drastically cut cycle times. In such environments as these, variances would not be insurmountable obstacles.

Gene Bylinsky. "America's Elite Factories," *Fortune* (August 14, 2000). http://www.fortune.com/index.jhtml?channel=print_article.jhtml%doc_id=00000743.

unit. For example, if we increase the number of letters typed by 10, total cost increases by $50 (10 × $5). Dividing the $50 increase by the 10-letter increase in activity gives us the variable cost of $5/letter. The cost per unit of a variable cost does not change in response to changes in activity.

It is not easy to determine a per-unit amount for fixed costs because total fixed costs do not change when activity is changed. The payroll department manager's salary, perhaps $75,000, is the same at 50,000 let-

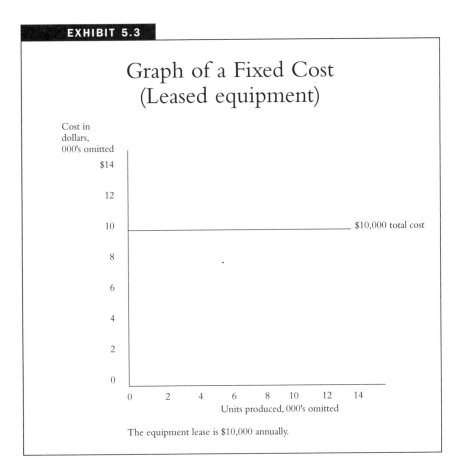

EXHIBIT 5.3

Graph of a Fixed Cost (Leased equipment)

Cost in dollars, 000's omitted

$10,000 total cost

Units produced, 000's omitted

The equipment lease is $10,000 annually.

ters as at 55,000. In fact, the fixed cost per unit of activity changes each time total activity changes, as illustrated below and in Exhibit 5.4. (These illustrations include the unrealistic assumption that the entire salary relates to letters processed.)

$75,000 salary divided by 50,000 letters = $1.50/letter.

$75,000 salary divided by 55,000 letters = $1.36/letter.

$75,000 salary divided by 65,000 letters = $1.15/letter.

$75,000 salary divided by 75,000 letters = $1.00/letter.

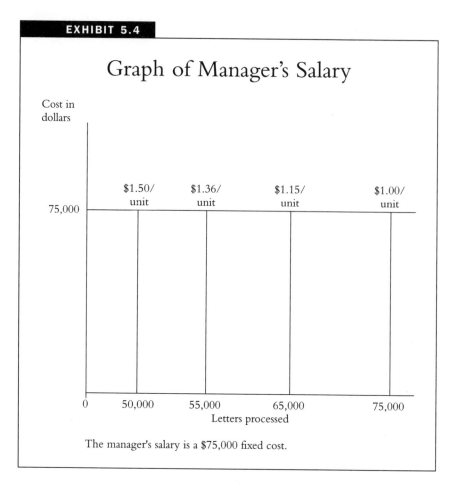

EXHIBIT 5.4

Graph of Manager's Salary

Cost in
dollars

75,000

$1.50/
unit

$1.36/
unit

$1.15/
unit

$1.00/
unit

0   50,000   55,000   65,000   75,000

Letters processed

The manager's salary is a $75,000 fixed cost.

Because fixed costs are not directly affected by specific activities as variable costs are, fixed costs must be assigned or allocated to units of activity in an arbitrary way. If, at the beginning of the year, the budget for the payroll department included a $75,000 salary for the department manager, the cost per letter or check can be determined only arbitrarily. Since the manager's salary pays for managing not only correspondence, but also preparing checks and perhaps performing other activities, we must first divide the salary among those areas. How much of the manager's salary should be allocated to letters? To checks? To other activities?

Allocating Fixed Costs

Let's say a consultant watches the manager and determines that 20 percent of the manager's time is devoted to supporting letter writing and processing, 30 percent to weekly payrolls, and 50 percent to various other activities (perhaps the preparation of checks for salaried personnel). Using the previously budgeted activity levels of 50,000 letters and 100 checks each week (or 5,200 per year), per-unit amounts are as follows:

Letter writing and processing:

$75,000 × .20 = $15,000 divided by 50,000 letters

= $0.30 salary/letter

Payroll check preparation:

$75,000 × .30 = $22,500 divided by 5,200 checks

= $4.33 salary/check

(Other activities are assigned the remaining $37,500 [$75,000 × .50].)

The salary/unit amounts we calculated are affected by changes in volume. What if the company started a second shift, adding another 100 workers—would the cost still be $4.33/check written? Probably not. The manager's salary might well stay the same, regardless. Likewise, the proportion of the manager's effort (however measured) necessary to process the weekly payroll might increase only a small amount, if at all. (After all, the manager is responsible for managing the check-writing process, not creating the checks.) In all likelihood, the manager's salary per check at 200 checks per week would simply be half what it was at 100.

But these are all arbitrary unit costs. Suppose a second consultant divided the manager's salary not by time (as the first did) but by the importance of the activity in the manager's job description and apportioned 5 percent for correspondence, 50 percent for weekly payrolls, and the remainder to other responsibilities. If we recalculate the per unit costs budgeted for 50,000 letters and 5,200 checks, we get completely different charges. The choice, we stress, is arbitrary.

$75,000 × .05 = $3,750 divided by 50,000 letters

= $0.075 salary/letter

$75,000 × .50 = $37,500 divided by 5,200 checks

= $7.21 salary/check

(Other activities are assigned the remaining $33,750 [$75,000 × .45].)

Fixed Cost Budget Variance

When a manager actually incurs more or less than the total budgeted amount for the fixed cost, the manager has an unfavorable or favorable budget variance. Budget variances are straightforward: Favorable variances are generally signs of efficient, effective cost management and increase net income. Unfavorable variances, conversely, are indicative of inefficient, ineffective cost management and reduce net income.

If property taxes are budgeted at $20,000, but due to an unexpected vote in the legislature, are increased to an actual cost of $24,000, the company has an unfavorable budget variance of $4,000.

Budgeted cost	$20,000
Actual cost	24,000
Budget variance	$ 4,000 unfavorable

Managers must investigate to find and, if possible, remedy the causes of unfavorable fixed cost variances. In this case, an increase in property taxes is beyond management's control.

Setting Standards

Managers sometimes set standards based on results obtained in the past, perhaps adjusted for inflation or a change in operating methods. But, using historical results to set standards tends to perpetuate the inefficiencies of the past by incorporating them in expectations about the future.

Time-and-motion studies and other engineering methods are frequently used to set labor standards. Engineers may also set equipment maintenance standards or establish specifications for materials in a manufacturing operation. Such approaches do not use historical data but may set standards using unattainable engineering ideals.

Perhaps the best method is to use the judgment of the managers who must meet the standards in a participative standard-setting process. This may create standards that are more realistic than idealistic. Managers who help set standards are generally more committed to meeting them.

Summary

When managers are evaluated according to what they are responsible for controlling, there must be a way to measure when they have not met expectations. And there must be a way to identify why their performance did not meet expectations. A number of variances have been developed to aid in this evaluation process. The market size variance will help identify when revenues and profits have been affected by a change in the market (a factor probably outside the manager's control). The manager's performance can be assessed by analyzing such variances as the market share variance (since a manager can certainly strive to obtain a bigger share of the market), the sales price, and sales collections variances (since the manager can affect pricing and cash collection policies).

Managers not only control circumstances related to revenues and cash collections, they also may control costs. Price and quantity variances are useful in evaluating management's control over raw materials or labor or fixed costs. Management can identify where a variance occurs and then investigate why it occurred.

CHAPTER 6

ROI and Investment Centers

After reading this chapter, you will be able to

- Understand the characteristics of an investment center
- Understand the advantages and disadvantages of decentralized management versus centralized management
- Understand alternative means of setting transfer prices

Calling a segment of the company an *investment center* seems like a great idea. Managers are often eager to designate segments of the company as investment centers and use ROI for performance evaluation and control. But before top managers designate an operation as an investment center, they should be sure it has four important characteristics:

1. Autonomous operations

2. Free access to vendors and customers

3. Separate revenues and costs

4. Management design

Autonomous Operations

Managers must be certain that a segment is an independent operating unit before they can gain the benefits of an investment center. The manager of the segment must control most operating decisions, subject only

EXHIBIT 6.1

Geographic Decentralization with Production in Each Location

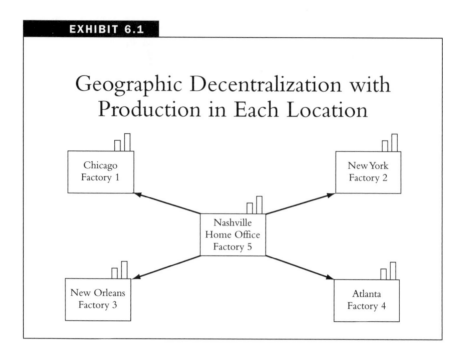

to broad policy guidance from top management. The segment manager must control—completely or in large measure—investment in capital assets, their maintenance schedules, production volumes, product mix, and prices.

Manufacturing operations, retail and wholesale outlets, and customer service and repair centers are examples of segments where this level of independent operating control is possible. Segments such as advertising departments, internal maintenance departments, and personnel usually cannot be independent in the same way and, therefore, cannot be investment centers evaluated by ROI.

Autonomous operating units are common to decentralized companies, although complete decentralization is not a prerequisite for independent segments. The intuitive image of a decentralized company is one with geographically dispersed branches (as in Exhibit 6.1), but decentralized management does not require physically separate operating segments. Decentralized management delegates decision-making authority to lower levels of operating management, as shown in Exhibit 6.2. These managers are often more responsive than headquarters to the conditions in their operating units.

In a company using a centralized management approach, top management retains direct control of operations; lower levels of management do not make major decisions. The advantages and disadvantages of decentralized and centralized management are in Exhibits 6.3 and 6.4.

Free Access to Vendors and Customers

An investment center manager must have free access to suppliers and markets, both inside and outside the company. The manager must be

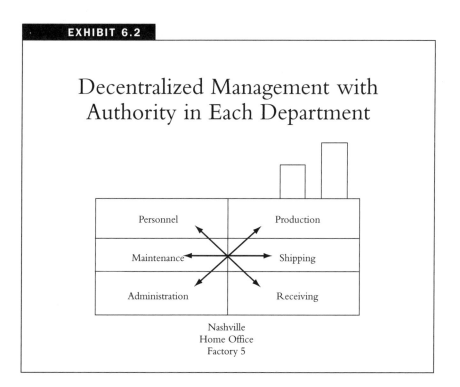

EXHIBIT 6.2

Decentralized Management with Authority in Each Department

Personnel	Production
Maintenance	Shipping
Administration	Receiving

Nashville
Home Office
Factory 5

EXHIBIT 6.3

The Advantages and Disadvantages of Decentralized Management

ADVANTAGES

Quicker decisions

Because details are not required to travel up
and down the management pyramid, decisions
are made more quickly.

More responsive decisions

Decisions made by operating managers are
often more responsive to current conditions.

More specialization

Operating managers focus on operations
and top management on strategic planning.

Improved motivation

Managers who participate in decisions are
better motivated than those who enforce
directives from headquarters.

DISADVANTAGES

Suboptimization

Individual segment managers may maximize their
own separate profits rather than working
for the good of the company as a whole.

Performance evaluation

It is difficult to evaluate the performances of individual
operating managers whose activities are different.

able to barter for the lowest cost when buying and must demand the best price when selling. For example, the manager of a segment that uses copper wire must be free to buy from the company's copper-wire production segment, or, if price, quality, or service are better, from outside the company. The same conditions must apply to the copper production

EXHIBIT 6.4

The Advantages and Disadvantages of Centralized Management

ADVANTAGES

Better control

Centralized management can easily
focus on a clear corporate goal.

Economies of scale

One large operation is often more
efficient than several smaller, decentralized operations.

DISADVANTAGES

Increased complexity

Large, centrally controlled entities that combine several
different operations are often complex and hard
to manage effectively.

Diseconomies of scale

Large operations are often more difficult to control
and keep efficient than are several smaller,
decentralized operations.

Span of control

The larger an operation grows, the more
difficult it is to control everything from the top.

segment (if it is to be an investment center). That segment must be able to sell its wire outside the company if a better price is offered.

Restricting segment managers to buying or selling to particular units within the company prevents them from being free to improve their return, a situation that can reduce morale and incentive. With free access to suppliers and markets, each autonomous segment will find the most efficient, effective, and economical methods for purchasing, production, and marketing.

When segments are free to purchase both inside and outside the company, segments that do a poor job competing with markets or suppliers outside the company will not survive. If the copper-wire operation cannot successfully produce copper wire and sell it to the downstream segment in competition with outside producers, the company as a whole is better off discontinuing the operation.

Separate Revenues and Costs

An investment center must be able to separate its costs and revenues from the rest of the company. Without this ability the segment cannot determine a profit *return*. If a segment *sells* its production to another segment in the same company, there might be a degree of arbitrariness to the selling or transfer price established between the two operations. If the production is specialized, perhaps tailormade for use in the downstream division's operation, there may be no realistic way to set an objective price. This problem is discussed later in the chapter.

Management Design

Management must consider the objectives of a segment and decide that the segment will be most focused on its objectives if it operates as an investment center. For example, assume a molding operation receives its molding compounds from an upstream department, molds the compounds into reinforced components, then sells (transfers) the components to a downstream department for use in a finished product. There are alternative sources for the molding compounds and alternative customers to whom the molding operation could sell its production. Thus, the molding operation could operate as an investment center.

But suppose top management wants the molding operation to perform a research and development function, both by conducting test runs using experimental molding compounds and by molding experimental component designs for the downstream department. The managers of the segments could negotiate in the market for the research and development services performed by the molding department, but trade secrets might be stolen and, even at a premium, experimental work might not be given high priority outside the company.

In such circumstances, management might not intend for the molding operation to place its highest priority on earning a profit but, rather, to gain its value in part from its R & D role, as illustrated in Exhibit 6.5. Thus, the molding department is best managed as a service center, not an investment center.

EXHIBIT 6.5

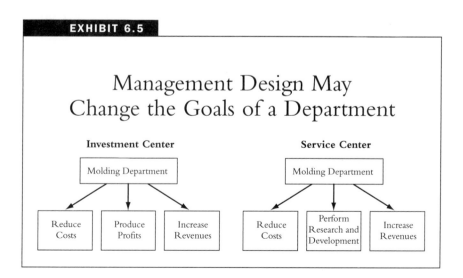

Management Design May Change the Goals of a Department

Other segments might completely lose their usefulness operating as an investment center. The company might, for instance, employ high-powered experts in its market research department who are capable of operating as an autonomous consulting group, offering services to clients in and out of the company. But to undertake market research in this way defeats the purpose of the department. The operating objective of the market research group must be to improve the market position of the company, not create a segment profit. The same is true of the legal department, public relations, and other service departments.

ROI and Transfers between Segments

Investment centers must have separable revenues and costs. This is not a problem when there are alternative vendors and customers outside the company. In such cases, segments buy, sell, and transfer products from one to the other at competitive market prices. As a result, companies invest in activities that promise to generate the best returns. Conversely, if a segment grows inefficient and cannot operate in competition with producers outside the company, it will find no customers for its output inside or outside the company. Then it cannot continue. Investments in unprofitable operations are moved to profitable operations. If a segment competes successfully with suppliers outside the company, it finds customers for its output and its profitability justifies requests for additional capital or other support.

When there is no alternative vendor or customer and no true market reference price, problems can arise. In this situation, managers often create pseudomarket transfer prices based on several different general models. All these attempts to contrive an artificial measure to replace market price have the potential to cause problems and reduce ROI.

The six most common problems associated with transfer prices other than a competitively set market price are as follows:

1. Misdirected capital investments made based on artificial returns

2. Misdirected operating funds because budgets are based on artificial cost and revenue figures

3. Bonuses and other performance rewards based on assessments using negotiated or mandated results, rather than real costs and revenues

4. Erroneous actions resulting from evaluations of problems and opportunities distorted by ignorance of true revenues and costs, including opportunity costs

5. Inappropriate responses to changes in markets and competitors due to costs and revenues that do not reflect these processes

6. Poor morale among segment managers, resulting from perceptions of differential treatment

Transfer Prices

Transfer prices used in place of actual market prices established in competition with producers outside the company vary greatly in their usefulness and their potential for harm. There are four methods of setting transfer prices that are in wide use.

Published Market Prices

Many companies that do not allow segments to buy or sell outside the company use published market prices to transfer intermediate products between segments. Published market prices are also adapted for use as transfer prices when the actual intermediate product is a different (perhaps custom-made) type, grade, or quality than the products whose prices are published.

Often, published prices of intermediate products are for different quantities of product, in a different location, than the product transferred. Published prices are usually spot prices, rather than long-term

Transfer Pricing

Transfer pricing can be a thorny issue, as shown by the following anecdote from "Sandy Weill's Monster" in *Fortune*.

> In an institution that promotes cross-selling, for example, there is always the question of how the financial spoils are divided up between the two divisions—a matter that goes under the name *transfer pricing*. For example, suppose that a Salomon Smith Barney financial consultant sells a mutual fund "manufactured" by Citi's investment management division. What's the price that the IM division receives? The answer, since it determines profit, is extremely important to executives getting paid (and paying their people) according to what their own bottom line looks like. One former Citi executive says that difficult questions like these have sometimes aggravated business heads to the point of their "barely speaking to each other."
>
> Asked about transfer pricing pains at Citi, Weill says testily that he wishes people "would think about doing the business first, and worry about who gets the credit second." But, trying to mediate, he also has his financial people studying plans for internally double-counting revenues so as to make profits (or losses) accrue to both parties involved in a cross-selling event. He adds that the weekly meeting of the business heads has the potential—he obviously hopes—to smoothe disagreements like those about cross-selling, because it encourages these people to "relate."

Loomis, Carol J. "Sandy Weill's Monster." *Fortune* (April 16, 2001). http://www.fortune.com/indexw.jhtml?channel=artcol.jhtml&doc_id=201176&page=4D/

contract prices more suitable to the relationship between a company's segments. Adjustments are made for these differences.

Published spot price	$107
Quality upgrade	12
Quantity discount	(9)
Shipping cost adjustment	5
Sales commission saving	(20)
Required packaging	22
Transfer price	$117

It is a good idea to use published market prices either directly or adjusted for differences. Such prices realistically approximate the prices that would be obtained in a competitive transfer pricing system.

Marginal Cost

Marginal cost is the additional cost required for a segment to produce an additional unit of product or service. Most frequently, this is raw material and labor, plus whatever components of overhead costs (such as electricity or lubricant) are increased when additional units are produced. (Most overhead costs are related to the capacity to produce and do not increase when additional units are produced. Examples include property taxes, lease payments, and supervisory salaries.)

Materials used:		
Metal	$46	
Hinges	4	
L-brackets	24	$ 74
Labor used:		
Assembly hours 2 × $36		72
Marginal overhead		82
Transfer price		$228

EXHIBIT 6.6

Transfer Prices and Profit

Type of Transfer Price	Amount of Transfer Price	Total Cost per Unit	Profit (Loss) per Unit
Marginal cost	$228.00	$336.00	($108.00)
Full cost	$336.00	$336.00	0.00
Marginal cost plus markup (65%)	$376.20*	$336.00	$40.20
Full cost plus markup (30%)	$436.80**	$336.00	$100.80

* $228 × 1.65 = $376.20.
** $336 × 1.30 = $436.80.

Marginal costs are useless in calculating profit produced by the segment producing the transferred product because the total cost of production will always include capacity costs above the marginal cost of production (as illustrated in Exhibit 6.6 and the full-cost example that follows). Marginal cost provides information useful for short-term operating decisions such as pricing for special orders or promotions. A special order or promotion should not be priced below the total marginal cost of production in all segments unless the company is willing to sustain a loss.

Perhaps the biggest disadvantage of marginal cost as a transfer price is that production inefficiencies are hidden and passed to downstream segments. The inefficiencies of one segment are masked by the efficiencies of the next.

Full Costing

Full cost is the total (full) cost required for a segment to produce a product or service, consisting of raw material, labor, and an allocated portion of all overhead costs (including capacity costs that do not increase when additional units are produced).

Materials used:		
Metal	$46	
Hinges	4	
L-brackets	24	$ 74
Labor used:		
Assembly hours 2 × $36		72
Full overhead per unit		190
Transfer price		$336

Full costs also are useless in calculating profit produced by the segment producing the transferred product, because the total cost of production will be approximately equal to the transfer "revenue." Again, see Exhibit 6.6. Unlike marginal costs, full cost does not provide information useful for short-term operating decisions, but is important in pricing production in the normal course of business. A product must be priced above the total full cost of production in all segments if the company is to earn a profit.

The biggest disadvantage of full cost, like that of marginal cost, is the potential for inefficiencies to be hidden and passed to downstream segments.

Markups on Cost

To make cost-based transfer prices appear more useful, many companies add an arbitrary profit markup. The markup can be applied to marginal or full cost, as illustrated in Exhibit 6.6. Using a markup on cost allows a segment manager to prepare an income statement, show a profit, and report an ROI. For all appearances, cost-plus transfer prices perform like true-market price-transfer prices. Except they do not.

Cost-plus transfer prices do not bring the discipline of competition to producing segments. They are authoritarian and arbitrary, most commonly

Transfer Pricing

There are various cost-based or otherwise formula-driven transfer prices, but scholars tend universally to recommend having market-based transfer prices or none at all. When there is no market price to use as a guide in setting transfer prices, using cost-based, formula-driven transfer prices can cause managers to take dysfunctional actions, contrary to the company's overall best interests. Excess costs, for example, can be passed along to other divisions with impunity. When the markup is a percentage of cost, inefficient, inflated costs increase the transferring manager's *profits*. However, in the real world, companies use cost-based, formula-driven transfer prices every day, in spite of the best theory.

set by top management using a markup return based on the company's ultimate gross profit on sales when it sells to customers outside the company, or some measure of the company's or the segment's cost of capital. Another approach to setting segment markups is to allow segment managers to earn the profit they think would be necessary when selling to an outside customer. Neither approach creates a competitive market price.

Summary

The use of ROI to control and evaluate performance for an investment center can be a great idea. However, it is important to make sure that investment centers have certain characteristics. The center should be an independent operating center with the manager in a position to make most of the operating decisions.

The center should be free to buy and sell wherever the manager thinks is most efficient and effective. The center's costs and revenues should be separable from the rest of the company in order to determine the segment's profit. In situations where investment centers within a company buy and sell to each other, it is necessary to set appropriate prices for these exchanges. Such transfer prices can be determined in a variety of ways, including use of market prices, marginal costs, full costs, and cost plus a markup.

CHAPTER 7

Return on Technology Investment: ROTI and ROIT

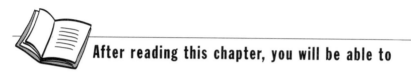

After reading this chapter, you will be able to

- Understand operations technology and infrastructure technology

- Use the value chain approach to analyze the impact of technology investments

- Evaluate the impact of technology investment on upstream and downstream links in the value chain

- Find available vendor models to estimate the ROI of a technology investment

- Evaluate the effect of technology on a basic business process by determining process objectives and metrics and the effect of technology on the process

- Understand the basic components of return on infomation technology, or ROIT: investment, costs, and benefits

- Determine the payback or return on a technology investment (ROTI)

- Calculate the dollar-impact of an improvement in productivity

Determining the expected or actual ROI for technology investments is problematic. Often the return consists of intangible benefits that may not be readily measured or even identified as resulting directly from a specific technology investment. Federal Express invested in technology that allowed customers to use the office computer to track shipments. Although the cost of supplying customers tracking information may be measured directly, what change in revenue or profit can Federal Express link directly to this investment? Often, the return associated with a technology investment consists partly or wholly of events that did not take place. For example, the return on an investment in a firewall consists of the savings from hacker-generated problems and losses that did not occur. How expensive might they have been? The return on an investment in a biometric security device must be measured as the avoided cost of intrusions.

Typically, the best evaluation metric for capital investments is a measure of discounted cash flows, net present value (NPV), or internal rate of return (IRR). But measures of discounted cash flow fail to capture strategic concerns and intangible, difficult-to-measure returns, such as customer satisfaction, manufacturing flexibility, or quality enhancement. Assume a company, for example, used NPV or IRR to select among several computer systems available to replace an old system. Assume, also, that one of the choices was, "Wait until next year." Moore's Law predicts that computers will double in power or halve in price every year to eighteen months. If next year's system reflected the predicted power increase, or price change, the choice would invariably be "Wait." But of course, the NPV/IRR evaluation in future years would choose "Wait" again, and perhaps again, and again—hardly a reasonable choice.

There is no standard algorithm or template for use in calculating the ROI for investments in information (or other) technology. Technology investments, particularly investments in information technology (IT), can be divided into two investment categories: operations technology and infrastructure technology.

An investment in *operations technology* creates or improves a link in an industry value chain and as such is a critical component of a company's operation. Examples of such operations technology investments include the Web-auction site eBay and the virtual bookstore Amazon.com. Investments in *infrastructure technology* become part of a company's infrastructure and benefit the company by enabling another value-added process to operate. Examples might include investments in an intranet or a telephone system. Returns on this type of investment are difficult to quantify. The following sections describe these two investment categories in greater detail.

Investments in Operations Technology

Unlike investments in infrastructure, an investment in operations technology does not create its value by enabling other processes. Operations technology enables a primary functional component in the company's industry value chain and generates returns directly. Amazon.com most certainly has significant investment in an infrastructure that supports the business processes of ordering, receiving, inventorying, and so forth, but Amazon.com has also invested in technology that enables its primary competency: marketing books and other items on the Internet. An operations technology enables a critical business process that could not function without the technology. Amazon.com could perhaps perform its generic business processes (ordering, receiving, inventorying, and so forth) without supporting infrastructure technology, but its Internet marketing could not operate without its operations technology.

Investments in operations technology are best viewed and evaluated as a strategic link in the company's value chain. The value-chain approach to evaluating the ROI of investments in operations technology enables a company to see the prospective investment from the holistic perspective of the industry's entire chain of activities.

There are two value-orientated approaches to measuring corporate performance: *value-added costs* and *value chain*. The easiest of these to explain is the concept of *value-added* and *nonvalue-added* costs.

Value-Added Costs

Using this approach, management attempts, first to designate all costs as either adding value or not adding value as viewed from the perspective of the customer. All costs in the value-added approach are related to some specific activity. For example, the cost of fabrication is related to fabrication activity, and the cost of inspection is related to inspection activity. Thus, fabrication adds value as perceived by the customer because without fabrication, there is no product to benefit the customer. Fabrication creates value for the customer and is a value-added activity.

Inspection, on the other hand, creates no value for the customer that would not be created during the fabrication activity, if the activity had been done correctly the first time. There is no value created for the customer when a fabrication error is made. The subsequent identification of the error by inspection does not change the value of the error, nor does rework to restore the fabrication to specification. (Rework is another nonvalue-added activity.)

An activity is value-added if it causes a change of state or the activity allows other activities to take place. Fabrication changes the state of raw materials by changing it into pieces that are component-shaped and prepared for assembly. Assembly is value-added because it changes the components into a completed unit of product. Assembly allows the product to be painted, and so on. Exhibit 7.1 contains a listing of selected value–added and nonvalue–added activities.

EXHIBIT 7.1

Value-Added and Nonvalue-Added Costs

Examples of Value-Added Costs

Fabricating

Assembling

Painting

Machining

Cutting

Polishing

Examples of Nonvalue-Added Costs

Inspection

Rework

Scrap

Set-ups

Billing

Paying

Collecting

Once nonvalue-added activities are identified, management tries to reduce the amount of the nonvalue-added activity. Ultimately, the nonvalue-added activity should be completely eliminated and its cost driven to zero. Technology investments often offer the best route to decreasing or eliminating a nonvalue-added activity, and, hence, the nonvalue-added cost. Converting fabrication to a robotics operation may result in products made to such uniform standards that inspection is no longer necessary.

The value-added approach to improving profits looks only at the company internally. As nonvalue-added costs are eliminated, by technology or otherwise, the cost of creating value is reduced and profit is enhanced. A corollary goal is to increase the value the company adds to the product so that the customer receives more value for the same price (improving the company's competitive position) or, better, at an increased selling price. The exacting standards of robotic manufacturing that eliminated the need for inspections may also result in an increase in the quality (value) of the end product.

Value Chain and Operations Technology

The value-chain approach considers all activities or business processes taking place between the creation of the raw material used in the product, and the final consumption of the product by the customer. The value chain of a paint manufacturer might look as shown in Exhibit 7.2. The first link in the value chain is an oil exploration company that drills a well in Kuwait and strikes oil, producing the raw material for the chain. The next link is the tanker that brings the oil to the United States so that a third link, the refinery, can process the oil into dozens of useful petroleum products. Several of these components are useful directly in paint manufacturing and others are sold by a chemical company (the fourth link) to a company (the fifth link) that manufactures polymers used in paint manufacture. In the sixth link in the value chain, these polymers are used in manufacturing paint. The finished paint is sold to a paint retailer who, in turn, sells it to a contractor who uses it to paint a house for a homeowner, the ninth and final link.

A company might perform all the operations in its value chain, or any combination of the links. For instance, the paint manufacturer might

EXHIBIT 7.2

The Value Chain of a Paint Manufacturer

Oil Exploration/Drilling

Tanker Transportation

Refinery Processing

Chemical Sales

Polymer Manufacturer

Paint Manufacturer

Paint Retailer

Paint Contractor

Final Customer

do nothing more than manufacture paint, or it might also have a series of retail paint stores that sell its brand. Frequently, the same company does the manufacture of both the paint and the polymer. Employees and managers in each link in the value chain must think of ways to increase value to the final customer. The refinery may alter its process to produce chemicals that perform better in paint, increasing the warranty the retailer can offer the contractor, and the contractor can offer the homeowner. The whole value chain benefits when better value is delivered to the final customer, regardless of whether the chain consists of one company performing nine functions, or nine companies each performing one function.

The value-chain approach encourages managers to think outside of the box. Investments in technology, whether IT or other technology, must be made with an eye on the whole value chain. Often, the benefits are not linked directly to the technology application, but may be second-, third-, or fourth-level linkages from the link applying the technology. For example, enhanced technology might allow the production of a polymer that does not have as strong a paint smell. The polymer might not sell for a higher price, or produce a paint that does—but it might allow the contractor to use the paint in more confined quarters with less customer annoyance.

Value Chain, ROIT, and Infrastructure Technology

In addition to an industry value chain containing all the separate links performing different activities, each company can be represented by its internal value chain. The paint manufacturer, for example, might have an internal value chain, as shown in Exhibit 7.3. The paint manufacturer might decide to eliminate the nonvalue-added activities of ordering raw materials, receiving raw materials, and storing raw materials by upgrading equipment technology, and adopting a just-in-time (JIT) manufac-

---

EXHIBIT 7.3

The Internal Value Chain of a Paint Manufacturer

Ordering Raw Materials

Receiving Raw Materials

Storing Raw Materials

Preparing Paint

Canning Paint

Storing Paint

Shipping Paint

"ROI: Made to Measure; Terminal Wellness," *CFO*, vol. 17, no. 12, (Fall 2001), pp. 31–32.

IN THE REAL WORLD

Example of
Internal Value Chain

As happens in an industry value chain, technology improvements in one link might benefit links several levels away. For example, Delta Airlines's internal value chain might in part be:

Schedule flight

Sell ticket

Check in

Board plane

Fly

Disembark

Delta has begun offering passengers wireless Internet service that allows passengers to retrieve flight information and schedules. At this writing, Delta is testing a system of upgrades that will let passengers reserve and pay for tickets online, and with the same system, use a virtual check-in that will let passengers bypass the lines at the gate. The IT improvements in virtual ticket sales and flight information will reduce paper and personnel pressures at gate check-in.

turing system. (Ordering, receiving, and storing raw materials adds no value for the final customer: The paint will offer the same benefit level to the customer with these operations eliminated.)

Technology has made possible tracing the costs of activities with a precision accountants only dreamed of 10 or 15 years ago. Managers wishing to improve profitability will often look upstream and downstream in the value chain, examining the company's relationships with its suppliers and customers.

Supplier Linkages.

To increase quality, or meet production deadlines, a company is dependent on its suppliers for quality, on-time delivery. Traditional managers and accounting systems evaluate purchasing based on the cost of the items purchased. Quality is considered, but if the purchasing department can buy an item at $12 rather than $13, that is generally considered good. Purchase-related costs other than the direct cost of units become part of overhead and are averaged over all purchases.

However, computerized accounting systems now allow tracing costs of specific activities related to purchasing's decision to buy from one supplier rather than another. Accounting systems can now track many financial and nonfinancial measures as surrogates for quality, reliability, and on-time delivery. Costs are first traced to the supplier, and then the supplier's cost is traced to the products purchased from the supplier.

The surrogate cost for quality might be the cost of reworking units that do not pass inspection due to raw-materials problems. Analyzing warranty costs can assess reliability, and the cost of on-time delivery (or the lack of it) is measured from the amount of expediting cost incurred. The $12 and $13 units above might yield further analysis, as follows:

Activity	Average cost per unit	
	ABC Inc.	XYZ Limited
Purchase cost	$12	$13
Quality (rework)	5	2
Reliability (warranty)	2	1
On-time delivery (expediting)	4	0
Total cost per unit	$23	$16

In addition to these activities, a company might analyze suppliers' credit terms offered (affecting the company's cash flow), the lead-time required for an order (affecting the level of inventory that must be carried), and whether customer service is available if needed. Studies of the additional costs related to purchases might reveal that when all costs are traced to specific suppliers, purchase cost per unit and a uniform overhead rate is not the best method for evaluating purchasing performance or choosing suppliers.

Customer Linkages.

Traditional function-based accounting systems assign customer costs averaged over all customers, often as a percent of revenue. Managers cannot use the cost system to distinguish between profitable and non-profitable customers.

Technology has resulted in accounting systems that track customer costs as dollars per order and analyze the value-chain link between a company and its customers. Customer costs are a smaller percentage of revenues for large orders, a higher percentage for small orders. Additional considerations include terms required, lead time of orders, customer service required, and the volatility of the customer's demand. Managers may also trace other costs of small-order filling, as small batch set-up, inspection, and so forth.

Companies can use the costs of different classes of customers to focus their marketing efforts and to decide on the level of surcharges where necessary. Banks have used this type of analysis to establish the account privileges and charges for different types of account. Profitable customers may be rewarded with special privileges and waived charges. Unprofitable account classes can be structured to pay their way through reduced privileges and account charges.

Infrastructure ROIT Model

Infrastructure refers to the basic structure of a business. ROI for any infrastructure component, technology-based or not, is usually difficult to quantify. What is the ROI, for instance, of the elevators and escalators? Of the climate-control system? RSA Security notes that infrastructure investments, in general, are not subject to ROI evaluation.[3] For example, a company does not base its investment in elevators and escalators on any projected return. These infrastructure components are simply recognized as necessary. For many companies, IT and other operations technologies can no longer be viewed as support functions, but must be recognized as essential business infrastructure components. Nonetheless, many IT directors and others wanting to make IT investments find themselves faced with the task of developing a quantifiable ROI, or, specifically for IT investments, ROIT.

The ROI model for technology investments is still evolving. Despite this, IT managers who request additional investment in technology are finding they must prepare an estimated ROI as part of the process. Often, expected ROIT is the single most important metric in the proposal. Thus, IT managers are faced with an amorphous problem, with many tangible and intangible costs and benefits that might be included in calculating an expected ROI.

Guidelines and Estimators

Guidelines for potential customers to use in developing or estimating a ROIT have been developed by many companies that market IT systems or components, including IBM, Cisco Systems, Microsoft, and many others. These guidelines are frequently available on the companies' Web sites and may be accompanied (or replaced) by an automated *ROI estimator* for customers to use in calculating ROIT. The ROI estimator leads a potential customer through an often comprehensive series of questions that probe the areas that might be benefited by a specific product or product class (servers, selling, security systems, and so on). Both the guidelines and the ROI calculators contain lists of tangible and intangible costs and advantages specifically related to the products marketed by the company offering the material, and might not be applicable in their entirety to decisions involving the purchase of a different class of assets.

Still, the models available from venders are useful in several ways. Often all or part of the returns associated with a particular technology investment may occur in another process, upstream or downstream in the company's value chain, or may derive from events that were avoided and are difficult to identify. A vendor ROIT models' value depends on how comprehensive the set of questions is and how well these questions cover the specific application. Regardless, guidance from venders is useful in at least two areas:

1. Providing an extensive list of events that, as a result of a specific investment, have financial impact, positive or negative

2. Suggesting default values/cost estimates for financial impacts that are subjective and difficult to identify

Lucent Technologies' Web site (www.lucent.com) contains Lucent's Telechoice ROI calculator. The calculator contains a listing of events that affect ROI and default values calculated by Lucent, presumably based on Lucent's experience. There are separate macros for calculating ROI for small business, medium business, and large business. For one area targeted in Lucent's marketing, managed security—small business, Lucent's ROI calculator offers (among other information) estimated Service Take Rates for clients of Lucent's customers for different services. The ROI calculator requires input for three years. For site management, Lucent offers take-rate default values of 40 percent, 45 percent, and 50 percent for each of the three years, respectively. The Lucent estimated default values for the percentages of customers who will take firewall access control are 10 percent, 12 percent, and 24 percent for three years. The monthly price per managed site should be $150 (the default value). The monthly price for firewall access control should be $50.

Potential system purchasers can accept the default values in Lucent's ROI calculator, or override them with their own input amounts. Once the

TIPS & TECHNIQUES

Value Chain

Check carefully to see what time period is used when returns are calculated on technology investments. Calculations of ROIT are frequently made for a period spanning several years because IT investments typically offer poor or negative returns in the first year. Rather than describing an investment as returning a negative return the first year, and a positive return thereafter, the investment is described as creating a cumulative positive return in three years.

For example, the default values for a small business in the Lucent Technologies Telechoice ROI calculator yield a negative cash flow of $3,005,675 in year one, then positive cash flows of $10,187,261 and $48,243,529 the second and third years, respectively, yielding a cumulative 504 percent IRR over three years.

input of likelihoods, events, costs, and prices is complete, the ROI calculator prepares pro forma income statements for three years, with an internal rate of return for the three years and a three-year net present value.

The Value of Performing a ROIT Analysis

Investment in IT is more frequently tactical than strategic. For example, when accounting spreadsheets first became available, companies that used the software received a definite advantage. The advantage was particularly evident in budgeting and planning. Companies using spreadsheet software could prepare multiple iterations of a budget at different activity levels—sales at $1 million, sales at $1.2 million—to see the effect on profits and costs. Sensitivity analyses that were difficult or impractical manually were simple to calculate using spreadsheet software. But, as time passed, spreadsheet software became less expensive and more common. Ultimately, automated spreadsheets were the standard, and companies that used the software no longer had an advantage. Instead, companies that did *not* adopt automated spreadsheets were at a definite disadvantage. As technology increases, failure to "get aboard" when a new development becomes available may result not only in the loss of a tactical advantage, but a failure to remain competitive.

Thus, it is important that the costs of making a new or improved IT investment be compared with the cost of not making the investment, in terms of lost tactical advantage and ultimately, competitive advantage. There is frequently the argument that it is better to wait on the next generation of whatever technology is considered and the feeling that when the next generation arrives, perhaps the company should not be happy with "old" technology. Nonetheless, however advanced the new generations become, it makes no difference if the company's old IT system still satisfies its needs.

Cisco Systems maintains that the evaluation process itself has benefits that make the exercise worth the effort, even if no new technology

In the Real World

Use of an ROI Calculator

Before deciding to use a particular vendor's proprietary ROI calculator to estimate the potential value of an IT investment, consider the vendor's history with the application under consideration. Study the ROI calculator model to see if it captures the types of benefits, savings, and costs relevant to your own company and its operations. Is the model as sophisticated as needed? Who created it? The vendor? A consulting firm? Do you need to add effects not considered in the model? Does the time horizon of the model match the pattern of your intended use? Calculating a five-year ROI might not be adequate for an application expected to be obsolete in three years. Finally, if two or more vendors offer ROI calculators, evaluate your application using each model.

is added.[4] Cisco is addressing an evaluation by a company considering the purchase of high-availability networking, but the benefits are sufficiently generic to apply to other in-depth system evaluations:

- A better understanding of the IT within company's business model and the costs and revenues affected by the level of IT performance

- Quantifiable data and metrics that managers can use in decision making and planning

- The ability to perform what-if analysis of the consequences of different scenario relating to the IT area evaluated

- A better buy-in to the mission and operation of the IT function by non-IT managers who must participate in an evaluation

- The ability to compare future performance to expectations, whether the investment is made or not

- An improved ability to react to unanticipated events that requires the use or involvement of IT

Measuring the Impact of Technology Investment

Measuring the impact of IT investment is difficult because so much of the effect of an infrastructure component is tied inseparably to the business operation or process enabled by the infrastructure. A business process is defined loosely as a group of activities addressing the same objective. Before accepting a list of events as measuring the impact of technology investment, managers should insist that the metrics follow directly from the activities in the business process and address one or more of the objectives of the process. Thus, metrics used to evaluate ROIT should be based on both the basic business process affected, and the related business objective(s).[5]

An example of a basic business process is *sales to customers.* A list of related business objectives would include *maximizing online sales to exist-*

ing customers. Potential metrics used to measure progress toward this objective include the following:

- Proportion of sales generated online
- Proportion of existing customers purchasing online
- Sales drop-off rate
- Repeat business rate
- Percent change in the size of the average online sale

This metric and others are described in Exhibit 7.4.

Once an IT manager has considered the basic process of making sales to customer, and has developed metrics to address the objective maximizing online sales to existing customers, an IT manager can ask such impact questions as, "What if we use encryption to secure communication with customers and accept orders with digital signatures rather than requiring them to print, process and mail an order form?" "What if we establish a 24/7 hotline to answer customer's questions?" "What if we establish a tracking system that will allow customers to track their orders online?"

Examining the expected impact of these questions on the metrics developed should assist managers in recognizing and quantifying the returns on the required investment. If, for example, establishing an online order-tracking system would require an additional $40,000 server but could be expected to double the proportion of sales generated online and increase by 50 percent the proportion of existing customers purchasing online, the IT manager is prepared to develop a range of expected returns and the metrics by which the returns can be measured.

The Components of ROIT: Investment, Costs, and Benefits

Three components are necessary to measure return on technology investment: investment, costs, and benefits.

EXHIBIT 7.4

Processes, Objectives, and Metrics

BUSINESS PROCESS

sales to customers

BUSINESS OBJECTIVES

maximizing online sales to existing customers

POTENTIAL METRICS

proportion of sales generated online

proportion of existing customers purchasing online

sales drop-off rate

repeat business rate

percent change in the size of the average online sale

BUSINESS PROCESS

sales to customers

BUSINESS OBJECTIVES

minimizing cost of acquiring new customers

POTENTIAL METRICS

percent of new customers online

cost of each new customer

BUSINESS PROCESS

sales to customers

BUSINESS OBJECTIVES

maximizing customer satisfaction

EXHIBIT 7.4

PROCESSES, OBJECTIVES, AND METRICS CONTINUED

POTENTIAL METRICS

number of incorrect orders shipped

number of help line calls

number of exchanges

BUSINESS PROCESS

sales to customers

BUSINESS OBJECTIVES

maximizing customer satisfaction

POTENTIAL METRICS

number of incorrect orders shipped

proportion of incorrect orders shipped

number of help line calls per sales dollar

number of exchanges per sales dollar

BUSINESS PROCESS

product development

BUSINESS OBJECTIVES

improve response to changing market conditions

POTENTIAL METRICS

order cycle time

order delivery time

product time to market

time to change product

EXHIBIT 7.4

PROCESSES, OBJECTIVES, AND METRICS CONTINUED

BUSINESS PROCESS

product development

BUSINESS OBJECTIVES

reduce costs

POTENTIAL METRICS

cost of materials

cost of services

productivity measures

BUSINESS PROCESS

purchasing

BUSINESS OBJECTIVES

reduce cost of materials

POTENTIAL METRICS

cost of materials

bids taken

comparative prices

BUSINESS PROCESS

purchasing

BUSINESS OBJECTIVES

have purchases arrive when needed

EXHIBIT 7.4

PROCESSES, OBJECTIVES, AND METRICS CONTINUED

POTENTIAL METRICS

shortage caused downtime

lead-time allowed

average inventory levels

inventory level at each orderpoint

This exhibit is based on RSA Security, PKI and Return on Investment, 2001, available at www.RSASecurity.com, pp. 1–3.

Investment

The required capital investment is perhaps the easiest component to measure accurately. The investment costs typically include one or more of the following costs:

- Hardware
- Software
- Facility modifications
- Training for employees
- Consultant's fees
- Recruiting cost of new employees

In a study of retail e-commerce, IBM classified the investment initiatives of online ventures as focused either short-term or long-term. Sixty-three percent of the companies studied had a primary short-term investment focus. These companies focused on immediate results and rarely made investments larger than projected cash inflows. The remaining companies had a primarily long-term orientation and focused on becoming profitable in one or two years, following initial short-term losses. Companies focusing on long-term profitability invested significantly larger amounts than companies with a short-term focus and received significantly higher returns. IBM felt retailers that stressed immediate returns damaged their business by focusing on short-term ROI.[6]

Benefits

IT investment typically addresses the improvement of a basic business process by accomplishing one or more of the objectives related to that process. The benefits may be measured by the metrics shown in Exhibit 7.4. The benefits of new IT investment might thus be tangible or intangible and may result in increased revenues, reduced costs, and/or losses avoided.

In discussing hardware for high-availability networking, Cisco Systems advises companies to include the risk of not upgrading hardware and, because of that decision, losing business from network outages. High-availability refers to *five nines* availability—systems that are available 99.999 (or greater) percent of the time. A company that is four nines or three nines is not competitive.

Costs

Like benefits, costs can be tangible or intangible, and can relate to success or lack of success in accomplishing operating or strategic objectives. *Intangible costs* are much more difficult to quantify than are intangible benefits. Lost revenue from a system outage that impacts sales, such as an Internet merchant losing sales, may be objectively estimated, but the cost of frustrated customers is difficult to quantify. The direct cost of replacing an incorrect shipment may be in the accounting records, but the cost of damage to the company's reputation is unknown. IT-related costs might include any of the following:

- Direct operating expenditures (as salaries or energy costs)
- Indirect losses (as lost revenue or changes in stock prices or debt rating)
- Direct losses (as lawsuits resulting from failure to perform)
- Lost or forfeited revenue (as from customer turnover)

When the costs of quality are measured for a total quality management report, experts believe that the true cost of a product's external failure is 4 to 10 times as great as the product's measurable external failure costs. A failure cost of $1,000,000 in the accounting records for replacing defective units shipped may actually cost the company $4,000,000 to $10,000,000 in total losses. Although the order of magnitude has not been studied, the same phenomenon is no doubt present in e-business failures.

Payback

Payback is a frequently cited metric used in making investments in IT. Payback is a simple concept: A system that costs $100,000 and generates $20,000 per year in profit or savings will pay for itself in five years.

payback period = investment/average annual profit or saving

Payback is not a preferred method for making capital investment decisions. Payback ignores the total benefits of an investment—will the $20,000 annual return continue past five years? An investment that will return $20,000 per year for 5 years has the same payback as an investment that returns $20,000 annually for 50 years. Likewise, payback ignores the time value of money. An investment that returns $20,000 each of five years has the same payback as an investment that returns

Payback and Risk

Payback is most applicable to risky projects where the time it takes to recover the investment is a primary concern. Someone considering an investment in an oil refinery in Iraq might require a quick payback before considering the venture. A company might see IT investments in a similar perspective, requiring a fast payback, because technology is progressing at such a rapid pace that today's investment may be obsolete in one or two years.

nothing for four years and $100,000 in the fifth year. Some companies attempt to avoid the last weakness by calculating a *discounted payback.*

Payback avoids none of the problems of calculating ROIT because the analysis requires identifying what must be measured and then determining the amount of the investment and the profit or savings derived from the investment. META Group Consulting (www.metagroup.com), with 1,200 clients worldwide, performed an ROIT study of intranet applications that covered nine vertical markets: manufacturing, education, services, utilities, health care, telecommunications, financial, retail, and media. The study performed discounted payback analysis, focusing on the following factors:

- Capital and expense costs to deploy intranets
- Savings derived
- Added business
- Quantifiable benefits to business processes
- Nonquantifiable benefits

The survey found that 80 percent of companies surveyed generated a positive ROI, demostrating that the benefits of an intranet application exceeded the cost of implementation.

Changes in Productivity

Improvements in productivity are an often cited metric for evaluating returns on technology investment. Determining dollar amounts resulting from a change in productivity is not straightforward, however. Productivity is measured as output per unit of input.

productivity rate = output/input

If a company, in fiscal year 1, generates $10,000,000 in online sales with hardware lease costs of $550,000, productivity of the hardware is measured as follows:

productivity rate = online sales/hardware costs

productivity rate (1) = $10,000,000/$550,000

productivity rate (1) = 18.18

If in fiscal year 2 the company generated $12,000,000 in sales with additional IT hardware lease cost of $50,000 ($600,000 total), is there an improvement in productivity?

productivity rate (2) = $12,000,000/$600,000

productivity rate (2) = 20.0

Yes, productivity increased from 18.18 to 20.0. But by what dollar amount? To determine a dollar amount, we must restate the productivity equation so that we solve for inputs rather than the rate.

productivity rate = output/input

(Productivity rate)(inputs) = output

inputs = output/productivity rate

Now we can compare the inputs that would be required in fiscal year 2 if we had performed at the productivity rate of fiscal year 1.

$$\text{inputs required} = \text{output (2)/productivity rate (1)}$$

$$\text{inputs required} = \$12{,}000{,}000/18.18$$

$$\text{inputs required} = \$660{,}066$$

Because productivity increased in fiscal year 2, an output of $12,000,000 was produced with only $600,000 rather than the $660,066 that would have been required at the fiscal year 1 productivity rate. The increase in productivity produced savings of $60,066 at an additional cost of $50,000. The $50,000 produced an ROIT of 20.132 percent.

Theoretical input required in fiscal year 2	$660,066
Actual input required	(600,000)
Savings (reduction in input)	$ 60,066
New investment	(50,000)
Savings from productivity increase	$ 10,066

ROIT = Savings/new investment = $10,066/$50,000 = 20.132%

Summary

Measuring the return on technology investments is not a straightforward procedure. Returns are often intangibles that are difficult to measure objectively, or may occur in parts of the value chain different from the link where the investment is made. Still, returns on technology investments must be quantified before many companies will allow technology investment. The value chain affords a viable approach to examining the companywide and even industrywide returns to be generated on investments on technology. For infrastructure ROIT, it is useful to develop objectives and metrics directly from the basic business processes. Once the objectives and metrics are developed, impact statements can be analyzed and investment-generated returns estimated.

Payback is a statistic useful in evaluating technology because it is a measure of exposure to risk in an environment where rapid change is expected. Increases in productivity are a frequently cited metric used to evaluate the success of technology investments. This chapter explains the algorithms for both measures.

CHAPTER 8

Residual Performance Measures: RI and EVA

After reading this chapter you will be able to

- Calculate residual income (RI) and residual income return on investment

- Understand how RI overcomes one problem associated with ROI

- Understand the determination of a company's minimum expected rate of return and be able to calculate the weighted average costs of capital

- Understand the rationale behind economic value added (EVA), Stern Stewart's proprietary measure

- Understand the modifications made to operating earnings and how the cost of capital is determined using EVA

- Understand market value added and how it relates to EVA

ROI is strongly criticized for peculiarities described in the preceding chapters. ROI affects a manager's decision to accept or reject new investment projects or to dispose of capital assets already owned. Managers are motivated to avoid (or dispose of) any investment (new or old) that has a lower ROI than the ROI of the company or segment as a whole, because adding such an investment lowers the overall ROI. Additionally, any single-factor performance measure, such as ROI, can produce dysfunctional behavior when a manager attempts to maximize the single-factor measure. For example, maintenance or other necessary expenditures may be delayed to increase a period's ROI at the expense of the company's overall health and the ROI next period.

There are two residual profitability measures structured to avoid the deficiencies of ROI and other single-factor measures. *Residual income* (RI) is a simple measure of the returns that an entity generates above a minimum required rate of return, often the company's cost of capital. *Economic value added* (EVA) is a much more elaborate measure of a company's ability to increase the wealth of its owners. EVA is a proprietary measure copyrighted by Stern Stewart and has recently received a great deal of attention.

Residual Income

Residual income is thought to avoid the incongruent goals of managers who seek to avoid projects that have a lower ROI than the company or segment ROI. Segment managers are often charged for capital committed to their segments. If managers are not charged for capital, there is, at least, a minimum or hurdle rate that investments are expected to exceed. This rate is frequently the weighted average cost of capital. RI looks at the profit contributed by an investment above its cost of capital or minimum rate of return.

RI is the income earned in excess of a minimum rate of return. If the manager of a company or segment that creates a ROI of 25 percent evaluates a new investment that returns only 20 percent, the manager may refuse the project to avoid decreasing the overall ROI. However, if an investment is evaluated using RI and a 15 percent minimum rate of return, the manager will realize that adopting the project increases total earnings. Here, the $6,250 increase in RI justifies the reduction in ROI.

	Before New Project	New Project	With New Project
Investment	$500,000	$125,000	$625,000
Profit	125,000	25,000	150,000
Cost of capital @15%	75,000	18,750	93,750
Residual income (above cost of capital)	$ 50,000	$ 6,250	$ 56,250
ROI	25%	20%	24%

One problem with using RI for performance measurement is that it is difficult to make comparisons among segments of different sizes. Large segments should generate larger amounts of RI than small segments. In these cases, using a budgeted or target RI for each segment compensates for size differences—but in those cases, a budgeted ROI that recognized the value of the 20 percent project accomplished the same thing.

RI avoids none of the problems of ROI discussed in the earlier chapters except the tendency to avoid an otherwise desirable investment because it decreases a manager's ROI. The problems defining profit and investment are still present.

Determining a Minimum Rate of Return

The minimum rate of return acceptable for a proposed investment is the rate of return a company would forgo by investing in project A rather than in alternative project B, assuming the projects are of comparable risk. This rate should equal or exceed the company's cost of capital. A company's *cost of capital* is the weighted average cost of all the company's debt and equity financing. It is the weighted average rate that results from obtaining funds at various costs from stockholders and creditors. The cost of debt is simply the effective interest rate of each of the debt instruments. The cost of stockholders' equity is the rate of return required by stockholders for the risk of supplying capital to the company. The weighted average cost of capital (WACC), then, is the weighted average cost of these funds and represents the minimum acceptable rate that an investment project must earn if the company is to pay interest to its creditors and provide its stockholders with their desired rate of return.

Calculating the Weighted Average Cost of Capital

If a company pays $20,000 a year in interest on a note with a principal amount of $200,000, the effective rate of interest is 10 percent ($20,000/ $200,000). Because interest on debt is tax deductible, this rate is adjusted for the income tax saved. If the tax rate is 35 percent, each additional dollar of interest costs the company only $0.65 because taxes are reduced by $0.35 for each interest dollar. However, companies often issue many different types of debt instruments, each with a different interest rate. Finding the effective interest rate for each of these instruments can be complicated.

Calculating the cost of stockholders' equity is even more complicated. Stockholders expect earnings from two sources: growth in share prices and dividends. One way to calculate the cost of stockholders' equity is to divide expected earnings per share by the market price per share. If earnings per share of stock is $1.50 and the market price is $10.00 per share, the cost of equity capital is 15 percent. Complications in the calculation arise because, like debt instruments, there are many types and classes of owners' equity. Stockholders might have different earnings expectations about each class of stock.

We can calculate a WACC using the previous data and a company's capital structure of 60 percent debt, 40 percent equity, and a tax rate of 35 percent. The calculation results in a WACC of 9.9 percent.

Weighted cost of debt   + **Weighted cost of equity = WACC**

$$\left[\left(\begin{array}{c}\textbf{0.10 interest}\\\textbf{on debt}\end{array}\right) \times [1 - 0.35] \times 0.60\right] + \left(\begin{array}{c}\textbf{0.15 cost}\\\textbf{of equity}\end{array} \times 0.40\right) = 0.099$$

Using the cost of capital as a minimum rate of return assumes that the company will continue to raise capital in the same proportions used in the calculation (60/40 in our example). However, strict proportions are difficult to maintain and the company might expect to change the ratio because it thinks a different proportion might yield a lower WACC. (As the proportions of debt and owners' equity change, the cost of debt and stockholders' equity will change, and the WACC will change: There is an optimum proportion that will yield the lowest possible WACC.) When managers expect to change the proportions of debt and equity, the expected proportions should be used to calculate the WACC.

A manager calculating a WACC must predict the proportions of debt and equity, and the cost that will be required for each component. Because of this, a manager might use a somewhat arbitrary minimum rate of return, feeling that benefits of improved accuracy are not justified considering the cost of the complicated calculations and the subjective nature of the assumptions. Frequently, too, companies will not use a single, companywide WACC or minimum rate of return. Different projects or segments of a company may vary in the degree of risk associated with operations. For example, drilling for oil at a new site might be much riskier than building a new refinery, and thus might be evaluated using a higher minimum required rate of return.

Residual Income Return on Investment

A few companies have used a performance index based on RI as a percentage of investment. This ratio is derived from a desire to have the benefits of RI and ROI in a single measure, but it fails. Like ROI, the hybrid measure appears to normalize unlikes and have intuitive meaning, but in truth the relationship is artificial and, because of this, gives rise only to contrived interpretations.

For the illustration used earlier, the ratio (which has no particular name) is as follows.

$$\frac{\text{residual income}}{\text{investment}} = \frac{\$56{,}250}{\$625{,}000} = 9.0\%$$

What does this mean? Only that residual income with the project is 9.0 percent of the investment base, down from 10.0 percent ($50,000/$500,000) without the project. Any additional interpretation is meaningless.

Economic Value Added (EVA)

Shareholders rely on information produced by accountants and on criteria such as earnings per share and reported net income. But it is the premise of the EVA calculation that both earnings per share and net income are distorted by accounting procedures and do not give a clear picture of a company's performance. Accounting measures, it is alleged, are intended to calculate earnings that are much too conservative. The resulting reported profits are intended to tell creditors the amount of earnings under the most pessimistic of interpretations. These earnings amounts are structured to inform creditors how well protected they are if the company becomes unable to pay its debts. Accounting procedures are not designed to create financial statements that provide investors an impartial assessment of how well the company performed.

Calculating EVA

The simple definition of EVA is *economic profit*.[7] Proponents of EVA maintain that stockholders are not informed by accounting measures of

Real Use of EVA

Since the EVA concept was first introduced, more than 300 companies have used it, including Coca-Cola, Quaker Oats, Boise Cascade, Briggs and Stratton, Lafarge, Siemans, Tate and Lyle, Telstra, Monsanto, JCPenney, and the U.S. Postal Service.

This information is taken from Joel M. Stern and John Shiely, *The EVA Challenge*, (New York: John Wiley & Sons, 2001), p. 16.

profit. Instead, stockholders need to know how successful the company is at creating new wealth. *Equity* is defined as *property rights*. There are two types of property rights, the equity of creditors (liabilities) and the equity of owners (stockholders' equity). EVA is said to measure in real terms the increase in wealth, defined as total equities—including both creditors' equity and stockholders' equity. EVA is the statistic that stockholders need. When bonus plans use EVA rather than earnings per share or ROI to measure the performance of managers, managers pursue activities congruent with the interests of stockholders. Change in EVA is the force that causes change in the market price of a company's stock.

The equation for calculating EVA is as follows.

EVA = NOPAT = (the cost of capital) × (total debt and owners' equity)

NOPAT is *net operating profit after taxes*. If a company's NOPAT is $3,000 and its total debt and owners' equity are $10,000 with a 10 percent cost of capital, EVA is calculated as:

EVA = $3,000 − [$10,000 × .10]

EVA = $3,000 − $1,000

EVA = $2,000

If a company earns only enough to cover its cost of capital, it has earned no profit. This is why the cost of capital is often a company's minimum desired rate of return: Anything less creates a loss.

The "net" NOPAT refers to the adjustments to operating profit after tax that must be made to arrive at NOPAT. NOPAT might well have been named OPATA—operating profit after taxes and adjustment. Proponents of EVA have found 120 separate distortions of profit created by accounting procedures. A correction is required for each distortion present in a company's income calculation to arrive at NOPAT, although most companies have only a few. The accounting treatment of the following items are felt to be the most egregious distortions of reported profits and its surrogate measures, such as earnings per share and the price/earnings ratio:

- *Research and development.* Accounting procedures require that investments in research and development be expensed each year, as though the expenditure would provide no benefit in future years. The simple definition of an *asset* is a cost that will benefit the future, an *expense* being a cost that carries no future benefit. EVA proponents argue that expensing research and development both understates a company's assets and overstates expenses, driving profits down.

- *Advertising and selling.* Accounting procedures likewise require that advertising and other selling/marketing costs be expensed when incurred. EVA proponents make the same argument that expensing these costs understates a company's assets, overstates expenses, and drives profits down.

- *Employee training.* These costs are also expensed, failing to recognize that the future is benefited by training employees. As a result, assets are overstated and profit is understated.

- *Historical cost.* Historical cost causes a different problem. Assets are shown in the balance sheet at their original purchase cost, or at market price, whichever is lower. With even mild inflation, this causes assets to be understated. If a company

EXHIBIT 8.1

Straight-Line and Accelerated Depreciation Expense

Year	Straight-Line Depreciation (1)	Sum-of-the-Years'-Digits Depreciation (2)	Difference (2) − (1)
1	$2,500	$4,000	$1,500
2	2,500	3,000	500
3	2,500	2,000	(500)
4	2,500	1,000	(1,500)
Total	$10,000	$10,000	-0-

purchased land on Main Street for $100,000 in 1912, and it is now worth $10 million, it is shown on the balance sheet at $100,000.

- *Deferred taxes.* Accounting procedures often include as expenses amounts of deferred taxes not yet paid by a company. Although these taxes might be liabilities of the company, they are not expenses. Deducting deferred, unpaid taxes depresses profit and owners' equity.

- *Reserves.* Accountants create many reserves or allowances, such as the allowance for warranty obligations coming due in the future, or for bad debts not yet identified. Often these reserves are too large and unnecessarily obscure profits. SEC Chairman Arthur Levitt, Jr.[8] has referred to such reserves as *cookie-jar reserves.* Proponents of EVA believe that warranty costs are better measured when a company waits until the cost is paid before recognizing the associated expense.

- *Alternative accounting methods.* Companies can frequently choose among alternative accounting methods, some of which affect taxable income. Exhibit 8.1 shows the difference between straight-line and accelerated sum-of-the-years'-digits (SYD) depreciation for a $10,000 machine with a four-year life and no salvage value. SYD depreciation yields higher depreciation expense and lower net income than straight-line in the first two years of the machine's life, but the situation is exactly reversed in the last two years. Over the machine's four-year life, both methods result in the same total depreciation expense and earnings.

Regardless of the depreciation method used for financial reporting, a company is free, for tax reporting purposes, to use the depreciation method that results in the lowest tax liability—so the choice of depreciation method for earnings does not result in different cash flows, only in different reported earnings. Other procedural choices require a company to use the same method for both financial reporting and taxes. The choice of inventory methods is an example of alternative methods that must be the same for financial reporting as for taxes. When the same method must be used for both taxes and financial reporting, the choice affects cash flows as well as reported profits.

Managed Earnings

Reported profits are also distorted by managers who attempt to "manage" earnings rather than operations.[9] Managers are motivated to increase profits, and the increase must be an acceptable size. The increase must be at least as large as stockmarket analysts have predicted. Missing analysts' predictions by as little as a penny can cause the company's stock price to tumble.

Managers can manage profits in many ways. Managers can increase reported profits by changing the timing of revenue and expense recognition. For example, a retailer might offer liberal credit terms to entice customers to buy who would customarily wait until next year. A company that advertises "No payment or interest until June" might motivate

LIFO vs. FIFO

We can compare Last-in-first-out versus First-in-first-out inventory methods this way.

If a company has the following inventory transactions:

Beginning inventory	1 unit	@	$10/unit	$10
Purchase	2 units	@	$15/unit	30
Total available for sale	3 units			$40

and the company then sells one unit for $20, LIFO and FIFO inventory methods give results as follows:

	LIFO	FIFO
In the income statement:		
Sales	$20	$20
Cost of goods sold	15	10
Gross profit	5	10
In the balance sheet:		
Inventory	25	30
	(10 + 15)	(15 + 15)

If the company must spend $15 (or more) to replace the unit sold, a company using FIFO inventory has cost of goods sold less than the cash required to replace the inventory sold. If the company uses LIFO inventory, the cost of the most recent inventory purchased is

customers to buy appliances or computers for Christmas instead of waiting until next year. Such shifts in sales increase current-year earnings but steal sales from next year. Earnings this year are increased, but earnings the next year are reduced.

Managers can defer discretionary expenses to improve current earnings. In other situations, managers can accelerate expenses to take the "hit" in a current year of expected low earnings and improve prospects for next year. Travel, maintenance or advertising expenditures might be delayed from December, year one, to January, year two, to reduce year one expenses. In early fall, managers might be able to set the date for repainting the equipment and factory buildings, or for the annual sales meeting. Delaying these expenses will improve current earnings; accelerating them will improve next year. Changing the timing of revenues and expenses produces an increase in current reported earnings that cannot be sustained in future periods.

Questionable Practices

Some efforts to manage earnings go beyond simply timing changes. Managers might increase sales through loose credit standards that also increase bad debts, or might bias expenses that must be based on estimates, such as obsolete inventories or warranty costs to delay recognition of the full amount of these expenses. Actions such as these are ethically questionable and result (if successful) in earnings increases in one year at the expense of another, as the costs must eventually be written off. Profits created by such questionable practices cannot be sustained and do not provide an accompanying increased inflow of cash or other assets. A study, years ago, by the National Accounting Association found that straight-line depreciation is the most appropriate method for most manufacturers.

Exhibit 8.1 shows the difference between straight-line and the accelerated SYD depreciation for a $10,000 machine with a four-year life.

Market Value Added

Market value added (MVA) is defined as the "difference between the market value of a company and the sums invested in it over the years."[10] If the market price of a company's stock is based on expectations about

IN THE REAL WORLD

LIFO Reserve in the Financial Statements

Some accounting distortions can be removed if a financial statement user knows how. A LIFO reserve is calculated by accountants and given in the Notes to the financial statements. The LIFO reserve is the difference between LIFO cost and the replacement cost of the inventory (usually assumed to be FIFO cost). Analysts can use the LIFO reserve to determine the effect of the LIFO/FIFO choice on the quality of earnings. For example, if ACME Company had cost of goods sold of $1,000,000 using LIFO and the inventory note to the financial statements shows a LIFO reserve of $150,000 in year FY 1, and $200,000 in FY 2, the increase in LIFO reserve from FY 1 to FY 2 is $50,000. Thus, if FIFO inventory had been used, cost of goods sold and, consequently, earnings before tax, would have been $50,000 higher, inflated by using the LIFO inventory accounting method.

the company's performance in the future, which is best measured by increases in EVA, then MVA is properly described as "the present value of future expected EVA."[11] MVA is calculated as:

$$MVA = (\textbf{market value of common stock}$$
$$+ \textbf{ market value of preferred stock}$$
$$+ \textbf{ market value of debt})$$
$$- \textbf{ total capital}$$

Summary

There are two important residual measures of corporate performance, residual income (RI) and equity value added (EVA). RI is much less informative than EVA and is used primarily as a method to atone for the problems inherent in ROI. EVA is a proprietary measure used successfully by many large companies. EVA attempts to calculate the increases in total equities (creditor and owner) each year. A number of adjustments must be made to profits to arrive at NOPAT. This amount minus the cost of capital (creditor and owner) is the equity value added each year. EVA results in a useful calculation of profits and keeps managers focused on increases in shareholder wealth. Market value added (MVA) is a companion to EVA that concentrates on the growth of a company's market value, as opposed to the growth of its equity.

Notes

The Importance of Return on Investment (ROI)

1. Roger Lowenstein, "The '20% Club' No Longer Is Exclusive," (Intrinsic Value), *Wall Street Journal* (May 4, 1995), C1.

Variations of ROI

2. See Ayres, "Perceptions of Earnings Quality: What Managers Need to Know," *Management Accounting* (March 1994), pp. 27–29.

Return on Technology Investment: ROI and ROIT

3. RSA Security, PKI and Return on Investment, 2001, available at www.rsasecurity.com.

4. Cisco Systems, White Paper: "Justifying Investments into High-Availability Networking," 2001, available at www.cisco.com.

5. This metrics discussion is patterned after and based on the approach used in the RSA Security publication previously cited, "PKI and Return on Investment."

6. answerthink and IBM, "e-Retailing Investment Strategies," a presentation, July 13, 2000.

Residual Performance Measures: RI and EVA

7. Joel M. Stern and John Shiely, *The EVA Challenge,* (New York: John Wiley & Sons, 2001), p. 15. Joel Stern is one of the principles of Stern Stewart, owner of the proprietary measure EVA.

Much of the discussion in this chapter uses *The EVA Challenge* as its primary reference.

8. Arthur Levitt, Jr., "The Money Game," (New York, September 28, 1998). Remarks at the NYU Center for Law and Business.

9. Id.

10. Stern and Shiely, p. 16–17.

11. Id.

Index

W